Everything We Have Unlearned

Recovering Resilience, Love, and Courage After Trauma, Grief, and Hardship

Sierra Frost

To contact the author or for information on bulk orders, send an email to
info@invitationwellness.com

Frost, Sierra.
1st edition.
ISBN: 978-1-0878-3689-8
Printed in the United States of America

Cover Art by Jackie Deblasio
Cover Design by Stephanie Ingram

Published by:
Boundless Media
PO Box 273178
Fort Collins, CO 80527

To my little girl,
as promised,
your truth is told.

To Fallon and Everly,
may you know the stories that come before you,
both told and untold,
and may you be brave enough to share your own.

Contents

1

"The privilege of a lifetime is being who you are."
-Joseph Campbell

"The trauma said, 'Don't write these poems.
Nobody wants to hear you cry about the grief inside your bones."
-Andrea Gibson

Dear Survivor,

You have spent a lot of time in your growing season. Don't forget to harvest when you have arrived at full bloom.

I am speaking from a radical state of being in our culture, claiming that I am not *in recovery*, but that I *have recovered*. People have told me this isn't possible. Therapists have claimed that people don't recover from childhood sexual abuse. We have an addiction to growth and development that states we must always seek the next fix for our brokenness, another piece of our wholeness, or a step closer to the unattainable goal of enlightenment. What if enlightenment is not an ending but a continuous practice, and what if we could claim that we are done with searching for the parts of us that are broken, missing, or stuck in evolution? I am claiming that.

Recovery for me is defined as a joyous homecoming process. For the last seven years, I committed wholly to my recovery. With every decision I made, I considered what it meant to this commitment. I showed up to the teachings of my body, mind, emotions, and spirit. I read books on self-help, attended workshops on manifestation, and collected certifications to heal myself and heal the world like my life depended on it. And maybe, at that time, it did.

The scientist told me that our cells regenerate every seven years, which means that the month my grandfather Ralph died was the same month my entire body was a distinct person from the one who told my family their own secrets. His departure from this earthly plane was my departure from our earthly relationship and thus the inauguration of my identity beyond our relationship here.

I spent almost twenty-five years cracking open my seed, growing roots, and making sure I would stay alive if I reached the sunlight. After breaking the soil, I spent seven years in my growing season, spreading wide and reaching towards all these modalities and pieces of information to become who I am and discover how I influence the world. I am done now. My growing season is over.

This book is a torch that represents the next season. I am bored of the idea that I have anything to fix or develop further. I was never broken. I am developed. I have unlearned the things that kept me from myself and now I get to enjoy the yield. I have been initiated into my harvest season and it is sweet.

This book is for those who come after me. It is a torch that illuminates within this harvest the power of those who are growing around me, for those who haven't broken the soil, and for those who will be planted by the seeds of my eventual decay. For my nieces, for the children I have adopted in my neighborhoods, for the students I have taught, and for generations that will come after me: use this work to expand beyond what I do. You are invited to stand on my shoulders and be more resilient, more compassionate, more brave, and more loving than I am able to be. Your responsibility is to take this and surpass me. This is the cycle of seasons. This is the coming of ages.

This book is for those who came before me whose shoulders I stand on now. I sprouted from your teachings, your DNA, and your stories, both told and untold. I listened to your legacies and I honor you by doing better—cultivating more resilience, bravery, and love to add to this world.

My grandfather told his story to me, and this book is our story together. Many of our ancestors did not have the opportunity to tell their stories. They are left untold, living in our bones and felt by our bodies. For human creatures, to share our stories and to show up for the stories of others—in body, in emotion, in mind, and in spirit—is a life force.

How to Use This Book

There are two parts to this book: a narrative and an invitation. The narrative is the true story of my experience with childhood sexual abuse and recovery. It is important to understand that this is my unique story and does not reflect all stories of a similar nature. I believe my family members did the best they could, and I love them for who they are and what I learned from them and with them. This story is an example of the resilience that humanity can have, and it is a story of hope for healing and reconciliation beyond what we may believe possible. Finally, you can learn what some aspects of childhood abuse, sexual assault, and interpersonal trauma can look and feel like.

I invite you to use this book to explore your own recovery deeper, support a loved one better, or bring a sense of humanity back into your life and leadership. It is important to know that I am not special. I do not have any superhuman qualities that have made it possible for me to recover. You will make some progress using the exercises and information in this book, and I recommend having a trauma-experienced professional accompany you on your journey. This will enhance your safety, help you heal thoroughly, and break the cycle of isolation that most of us experience. The most important requirement for the professional you choose is that they believe in you—healing will not occur without this faith.

I see you. I am you. Recovery is possible.

With Resilience, Courage, and Love,
Sierra Frost

p.s. If you feel called to reach out, please schedule a time in my calendar at www.SpeakWithSierra.com/

2

"Love is the weapon of the future."
-Yehuda Berg

When soldiers prepare for battle, they gather all the information they can about the environment and the people they will be fighting. They train physically, mentally, and emotionally for months or even years. They prepare themselves to be separated from their families. They cultivate as much courage as possible before heading into combat. This is how I spent my childhood.

I told my family I was abused as a child when I was 24 years old. I imagined walking into my grandparents' home; it was decorated with vintage teddy bears, an impressive collection of salt and pepper shakers from around the world, and a clock that sounded bird chirps on the hour. My grandmother Kay sat in her corner recliner where she crocheted afghans and watched the neighbors check their mailboxes between hockey games on TV. It smelled like a mix of old books, baked bread, and potpourri. There were bunches of carrots and rhubarb harvested from the garden soaking in plastic pitchers of cold water that took up the whole sink and half the kitchen counter. Gallon-sized white plastic buckets with red handles full of raspberries, blueberries, and crowberries for jam covered the island. Tiny bugs filled their bellies with the delicacies in the buckets.

Outside the house, the lawn was blanketed with flowers. Ralph loved to garden. He planted dahlias, columbines, poppies, peonies, and lilac bushes in the front yard. Colors faded from indigo, fuchsia, vermilion, and white, transforming into edges of sepia tones as they wilted. I imagined the sepia spilling onto the vibrancy of the scene, as if I could put this moment in the past before it even happened by transforming it into an old photograph in my mind.

As I approached the house, it transformed into the picture I held in my imagination. I was a warrior. Salmonberry juice warpaint drew focus to my eyes and was smeared over my forehead and down my nose. I adorned layers of Alaskan courage in the forms of a long woven bowhead-whale-baleen kuspuk, a tanned bear skin breastplate and forearm gauntlets, and a holstered belt made of walrus intestine. Polar bear fur lined my deerskin cloak, and I kept dry wearing salmon-skin leggings. My feet were warm in payaaqek: knee-high cuffed seal-skin boots sewn together with sinew. Bald eagle feathers lengthened my hair. Breakup season muddied my attire, battered from decades of wear. My holster was empty. I held all the power I needed in my voice.

To my left was a wild dog who resembled my first pet: half wolf, half husky, and wholly willing to protect me. To my right was my 4-year-old self. She was fearless and moved with a deliberate and unrelenting grace. She held a walking stick made of spruce-tree root and wore a tiara braided from fresh alder branches with catkins dangling around her head, as well as a cape that dragged behind, leaving a trail of burning alpenglow in her wake. We were followed first by my ancestors: my mother's parents whom I never met, entire camps of Native Americans, generations of farmers from Illinois, Navy sailors from the California coast, merchant Marines and working-class Canadians, and Anglo-Saxons of England. After them were characters of strength such as Joan of Arc, Mother Teresa, Gandhi, Nelson Mandela, John Lennon, Baroness Bertha von Suttner, and Jesus. Following were sufferers of violence including the Rotherham children; Dr. Martin Luther King, Jr. and the boys and girls of the Birmingham Children's Crusade; victims of The Great Leap Forward; and the billion women who are sexually assaulted worldwide each year. As we moved closer, my allies positioned themselves to surround the house, now made of stone. In each corner was a towering turret, with looming gray clouds above.

My army extended from the Spenard municipality to all of Anchorage, spilling into the Matsu Valley, down the Kenai Peninsula, and lining the coast as they held time still. Each member was unwavering. They felt the earth under their planted feet and pulled fortitude from beneath that extended as robust rays into the sky. They held their palms toward each other, communicating that they would hold this space together and for each other in a network of energy. I felt the infantry at my back, made eye contact with my 4-year-old self, and nodded for her to stay outside with our wolf-dog and her grandmother Gwen. She nodded in return and allowed a tear to drip down her cheek, as if to thank me for protecting her. I motioned toward the front threshold, gazed one last time at the teachers who have come before me, and inhaled their wisdom and composure before opening the door and announcing, "I need to hold a family meeting. Is everyone here? We can start in five minutes so you can get ready."

I left the front room to go to Ralph. He was in the back bedroom, tucked away in the corner of the house; he was the king in the throne room. I told him, "Ralph, I am really sick, and I can not keep living this way. I am going to tell the family that you molested me. I wanted to tell you that you can join me and be part of this or you can stay here, but it is going to happen now." I could feel his heart jump when his neck snapped to meet my gaze.

"I knew this day would come. Well, my life is over then," he pitifully responded. I remembered that kings can only see the view from atop their thrones. I took a deep breath to prevent myself from scoffing at his lack of empathy.

"It doesn't have to be. Families can come together and work through hardships. We can do the same," I stated this and questioned it at the same time.

"My daughter will never speak to me again. She is already mad at me. My wife will never touch me again. Can you wait to tell them?"

"No, Ralph. I am really sick. I can not live this way anymore. I need to tell them. I am not keeping any secrets anymore."

"You could just tell your parents and not everyone," he continued his attempt to engage what he had taught me about niceness and abandoning myself for my family. His offers were manipulative alternatives that prioritized his wants over my needs.

"I am not keeping secrets anymore. Not with anyone," I repeated, then presented his options: "You can come with me into the living room or stay here. It is your choice. I wanted you to know you can decide." He turned from me and paced into the corner of the room, stared vacantly out the window, put his hands in his pockets and started jingling the change inside them. This was a noise I had winced at my entire life. I left him and returned to the living room to ask if the rest of the family was ready to meet.

"I need a cigarette." My mom declared her stress response.

"Okay," I curled my toes into my boots, "maybe it can be a quick one, because I have been waiting for a while to talk about this." She walked through the kitchen, past the produce and out the back door. After a few moments, I heard her creak open the screen and call for my dad. She sounds distressed, and I immediately wonder if Ralph is also in the back yard, attempting suicide before I can disclose his secrets. I decided to check and walked into the back yard where my mom was smoking and seemed pained as she talked to my dad. I couldn't hear the conversation.

I said the easiest thing that came to me. "Are you okay?"

"You better not kill your grandmother," my mom accused me as if she needed to defend the family from my words.

"This isn't about Grandma. This isn't about anyone but me," I explained.

"Well, maybe you should think of someone besides yourself for once in your life," my mom continued to speak to me as if I was a threat.

"Mom, fuck you. This is the first time I am putting myself first. I will see you in the living room," I said without concern and turned to go inside. I sat in the chair next to the door. Kay was still in her corner recliner. My aunt Corinne was sitting on the couch with her partner, my uncle David. My dad chose a seat at the end of the couch and put the footstool out. My mom stood next to him. I tried to call my brother, Cody. He had agreed to be there over the phone but didn't answer. I felt a hint of abandonment and feared that I was facing the same rejection that had kept me in danger. Perhaps I could not do this. Perhaps I was not strong enough to tell the truth. I could still turn back. I could make something up or stay silent and leave. I didn't have to do this. I felt my stomach stir and remembered my 4-year-old self standing outside. I remembered the volume of people who had come before me, surrounding the space for me, and immediately sat up straight to preach a disclaimer.

"I want you all to hear everything I have to say before you respond. You may want to interject as I am talking, and I understand this, but I am asking you not to. I am going to tell you something I have had a lot more time to process than you, and for that reason, I don't really want to talk about it today, but I want you to know that I am open to talking about it, and after a couple days, if you want to call and talk about it more, I am willing. I am going to leave and stay with a friend after I tell you this. He is picking me up. I need to have space and give you space. I want to tell you that I think I know why I am so sick." I felt the energy pooling in my throat, and while I spoke in a soft, steady voice, the energy escalated as if it were a blood-curdling roar.

I started with a matter-of-fact battle cry: "For a long time—I don't remember exactly how long; my earliest memory is when I was two; until I was almost twelve—Grandpa sexually abused me." With those words, the energy from my throat escaped, creating a sonic boom that rang into the air around me, into the far reaches of the atmosphere, destroying the walls of the castle, striking buildings across Anchorage, creating a tsunami in Cook Inlet and Prince William Sound, echoing west across the Bering Strait toward Russia, north into the Arctic Ocean, east across Canada, and south toward the Hawaiian Islands. I became a trough of the destruction ringing from my mouth. I heard a sigh of relief from my little self outside as the stones crumbled around the living room. My army tensed to hold the space, stopping the ocean from destroying the area while exposing every speck of dust collected in the foundation of my family as the debris settled around us. I took inventory of the war zone I had created. My mom's eyes had welled up, Uncle David was still and grounded, Kay was subtly rocking in her chair, Corinne seemed to confirm the information in her head with mine, and my dad stared into the distance, seemingly unable to look at me anymore. Perhaps he was time-traveling. I feel my heart sink when I saw his face.

I continued, "Every time we got together as a family, this would happen. Sometimes it happened when we were all in the same room, even. I have been embarrassed and ashamed and I didn't know how to tell you. I told you, mom, when I was four, and that's how I learned it was not a game—"

"But this happened all those years? Was your entire childhood a living hell?" Mom interrupted me. I wanted to hug her in that moment. I wondered if I would ever be a mother. I wondered if I would ever know the pain of hearing my child tell me they were violated, that I couldn't protect them. I could hear the guilt in the form of defense in her tone.

"Please let me finish, Mom. Yes, it happened all those years. I have been angry at all of you for the last few years because I didn't feel protected as a child. Corinne, you called me when I was 19 and asked me about a specific scenario that you saw. I wasn't ready to talk, so I hung up, and I'm sorry I did that, but when I learned you saw it happening and you knew this whole time, I felt rage. I made a plan when I was 21 to wait and tell you all after you died, Grandma. I couldn't wait any longer. Someone asked me if I ever considered the possibility of having PTSD. It was like a bomb went off inside of me and my body felt like it would explode if I didn't open my mouth today." I shifted back into my role as the protector of the family. "I am going to see a counselor, and I encourage you all to do the same, if you want. I've had twenty years to process this, and I've forgiven him, and things will get better for me. Please do not go into the back room and yell at him—that will not help us as a family. I want us to come together and work through this together. I don't want to be angry anymore. I want a family."

"I'm sorry that happened, and it will get better," Aunt Corinne broke the heavy silence that followed two decades of pain.

"I know. It already is getting better," I responded, unwavering. "That is all I have to say right now. You don't have to stay here any longer." Aunt Corinne immediately escaped. In the moments that followed, I heard her screaming in the back room at Ralph. She yelled about how sick he was and what a monster he was for hurting anyone, let alone his own granddaughter and a child. She said he would find hell. I came to the rescue.

"Corinne, please stop. This doesn't help anything. It isn't going away now. It already happened. We have to come together as a family and figure this out. This isn't healthy for you or anyone else," I stifled the consequences for Ralph.

"Why are you still protecting him?!" She repeated the same phrase she had said to me over the phone when I was 19. She was right. David came and convinced her to leave the room. I sat there and comforted Ralph, again telling him how we would work through it as a family. I held his hand. I still acted out of the coercion and behavioral modification I was manipulated into performing as a child to shield him.

He told me again how his life was over. I thought to myself that my life was just beginning. My dad walked into the room and stared at us. I said hello. He was silent. He looked at Ralph. I could see the pain in his eyes as he stared in disgust. I knew, in that moment, Ralph morphed into something new, something evil and unspeakable, and that my dad no longer had a father. I wish I would have gone to my dad, but instead I simply witnessed as his gaze communicated that he knew his father had lied to him years ago when confronted as to whether he had hurt me. I watched as Ralph became dead to him; my dad would hate him for eternity. He then turned and disappeared from his father's life forever.

Deep inside me, I felt a sudden turn of disgust at comforting Ralph. I stood up and told him I was leaving the house and returned to the kitchen, where I found Kay obsessively wiping the counters clean. "Did everyone go outside?"

"Yes, I think they are smoking, probably," she gently smiled at me, hiding her feelings to protect me from concern. I found my parents and Corinne and David crying while they chain-smoked in the back yard.

"I am so sorry. Everything is going to be okay. We will get through this." They took turns repeating expressions of comfort as I hugged them goodbye.

"I am going to be fine," I confirmed each time, knowing as they spoke to me, they were speaking to themselves. "I am leaving now. I will see you later. Be gentle with yourselves." I went back through the kitchen and hugged my grandma, proceeded to the front door, picked up my suitcase, and stepped with a sigh into my new life. As my boots hit the pavement, my energy body was gently lifted into the air. I held the hand of my 4-year-old self and we floated toward the sky with our army of support as if it were the rapture. As we rose, my armor fell back to the Earth piece by piece and scattered in the yard amidst the rubble. For the first time in my life, I felt weightless. I knew in that moment that what I had done would change my family for generations. I knew the power of my truth was unparalleled as the clouds parted to allow room for the midnight sun. From that moment on, soft would be my new strong, peace my power, and love my weapon.

3

"We have come to be danced
where the kingdom's collide
in the cathedral of flesh
to burn back into the light
to unravel, to play, to fly, to pray
to root in skin sanctuary
We have come to be danced"
-Jewel Mathieson

Alaskan summers are the time for dancing. Summer is when everything awakens from the flatline of winter with lush vibrance. After solstice, the light switch is flipped back on and never turns off, making nature's colors illuminant through the night.

The house I grew up in was surrounded by a sprawling spruce forest. The front lawn was sequestered in the perfect oval shape to be my stage and catwalk. The footpath winding around it and up the porch steps was the grandstand. I danced and sang and changed outfits to public radio for hours on the lawn. Our geese would dance with me as goslings, but as they grew, they would hiss and chase me. I remember feeling safe, liberated, and joyous when I danced in my childhood.

I see my inner child dancing alone like this now; she is still jiving on her own. She is unaware of anything but her dance. It is her refuge and her church; how she protects herself, how she talks to God. When she dances, she can feel every micro-muscle of her body, and she feels empowered by the autonomy of movement. She has permission to spin and feel her home-sewn jumper swirl as the wind hits her thighs. Throwing her hands towards the sky, she shouts out her anger in songs. With sass, she puts her hands on her hips and shimmies to the ground. Giggles erupt from her free spirit as she promenades across the grass, and her hair whips her face and sticks to the edges of her mouth.

I come to her as my present self with open arms, and she prances to me—grinning, barefoot, and eager. She jumps into my embrace and we twirl, tangled together here in mixed time and space. She loves being held by me. When she dances with me, she remembers what safety feels like.

She asks if I can take her home—to my home. I answer, "Yes, we can leave if you want." We get in the car and drive down the dirt driveway, avoiding the sinkholes of clay. She asks, "Is the place we are going warm? But not too hot, because I can't breathe when it's too hot. And is there a beach? With an ocean I can swim in? I want to dance in the waves in my swimsuit. I've never done that!"

"Sure," I tell her, "I know a place like that. We can go there."

"I never want to come back home again." She states flatly, looking out the window away from me.

I pause to remember I am the adult now, and I offer her, "What if, before we go on vacation, we go back to the house? Just to explore what's inside?"

"No thank you. I don't want to," she says.

"Does it feel scary?"

"Yes, I can't move inside the house."

"Okay," I hesitate, balancing validation and

encouragement, "What if I go with you? I will hold your hand, and if anything scary happens, I will pick you up and protect you. I will never be out of your reach. Never."

She ponders for a moment, then says, "Yes. Okay. I can be brave—I'm even good at that! Do you pinky swear?" I do. We shake pinkies and I pull the car around at the top of Kent Street.

"You are brave," I wink at her.

She furls her brow for a moment and explodes in thought. "Oh! I know what we need! We need capes! Heroes have capes!"

I ponder this. "Yes, heroes often have capes. I don't have one in the car, though."

She looks distantly ahead, then to the lower left, bites her lip, brings her hands to her chin, and says, "Yes, we do have capes! You can use that blanket in the back seat because you are big. I can tie this plastic bag around my neck and pretend it is full of glitter."

"Okay!" I chuckle, "Just not too tight around your neck, and never on your head, okay?"

"I know!" As we pull back into the driveway, she agrees and declares, "Let's go." We join hands and she starts marching with her knees up to her chest. Looking up at me with giant chestnut eyes, she states, "Sierra, it's okay because we are together." I wonder which one of us she is talking to as she peels off two branches of the lilac bush, leveraging the porch step. Small fingers knot the branches into a circle and she announces, "You shall be queen and I shall also be queen, because we are the same person!" She laughs heartily and seems to be impressed with her smart humor and royal status.

"In the future, someone really important will call you Queen Frostine," I tell her.

Her eyes dilate as she shouts, "Yes! I can't wait to meet that person!" She crowns me first, then herself. Taking my hand again, she grips my pinky and ring fingers together tightly and breathes deeply. As she easily unlatches the gate, she states in a whisper to nobody, "Queens are always brave." Her eyes are focused straight ahead. She crosses the porch and smoothly steps over the rotted hole in the deck board to open the front door into the mudroom. I see her glance to the right and notice the rifle mounted on the wall, far above her reach. This was its home during moose hunting seasons. She kicks the scattered shoes back towards the wall and straightens her cape. I think I see some golden glitter spill onto the carpet. She opens the door and tip-toes onto the mat, investigates the perimeter, and looks back at me.

She points to the right. "Remember, that's where Mom taught us to rinse the lettuce from the garden and knead the dough for eggnog bread?" Without waiting for a response, she points to the left, "That is the heater we sit in front of every morning to keep warm while Mom makes breakfast." She continues through the house, gently pulling my fingers to keep me following closely. "There is the set of Wildlife Fact Files we read. My favorite one this week is the bush baby. Sometimes I try and make my eyes that big in the mirror, and then open my mouth and make fangs like the viperfish. I can't do it without laughing. Do you want to try it?!" I make eye contact, widen my eyelids as much as I can, and let out an unexpected hissing sound as I drop my jaw and spread my lips to show off my teeth. "Wow! You are so good at making faces! Maybe you should be in the circus someday!" She sincerely exclaims as she moves beyond the couch and toward her bedroom. "Cody lets me sleep on the top bunk and I love it because I feel tall! I have this blueberry pie I made from playdough and four math homeworks that Mom made me. I really want to go to school, but Mom says I'm not old enough yet, so I just go to preschool and she lets me do homeschool. I am teaching all the teddy bears like Mom teaches me. Right now they are practicing how to add numbers with the pie pieces. Katie is the best because she is the oldest." I recall the plush brown bear I was gifted on my first Christmas and witness with awe how creative, intelligent, and nurturing my 4-year-old self is. "These are my tiny colored bears. I won them at Chuck E. Cheese's. I chewed their ears off with my teeth when I was a baby. And here is the book that Mom is reading with us. It is called The Bible, and I don't really know what it's about, but there are animals, and I like the baby in it, and everyone wears robes all day long! And here is the blanket that Mom uses to wrap me in when I'm sick and coughing in the night. She picks me up and takes me outside so I can breathe and see the stars. I really like it when she does that—"

"Sierra, I noticed you are talking about Mom a lot. Where is she now?" I try to catch her mid-thought because I can see her avoiding something by showing me all the things I did when I was her.

"She is in her room." The silence that follows feels stiff.

"Do you want to show me that room?"

"No. Mom is mad at me."

"Oh. Do you know why?"

"I told her something yesterday that made her mad. Or it

was last week. Maybe it was Tuesday or Saturday. I don't remember all the days yet, but I can sing the days of the week song."

"What did you tell her? Do you remember that?"

"Yes," she stares at the floor. I can feel her freezing up.

"I won't be mad if you want to tell me. You know that I already know what it was. You are safe to tell me now," I wonder how successfully I can create safe spaces for my past self.

She closes her eyes and breathes deep, touches the crown still on her head, and again whispers, "Queens are always brave." After a moment to prepare, she tells the story. "I was late for bed when Grandma and Grandpa were here. I didn't know I was late. I brushed my teeth and put on my pink Barbie nightie and was walking to her bed because they were sleeping in our room, you know? And Grandpa grabbed me and started playing games with me. He was tickling me all over and I couldn't stop laughing to say I had to go to bed. Then he grabbed my ankles and flipped me upside down and started licking me. When Mom yelled from her room to see where I was, he put me down and I went to her. She asked me why I was late and I told her all of this about the game, and she was mad at me."

"So you think she is mad at you because you were late for bed? Did she say she was mad at you?"

"No. She didn't say that. She didn't say anything. She didn't get me in trouble. Her face turned red and her breathing changed. She told me to get in bed and she sounded mad and then she walked mad when she left the room and shut the door. I don't think I should talk about that game anymore. I just won't say anything when Grandpa plays it again. Then Mom can be happy and I can make her happy."

"Okay," I allow her to make this choice, knowing it already played out in reality. "I want to go see Mom with you now, will you come with me?"

"Why? She's not mad at you. I can stay here."

"She is not mad at me. I don't think she is mad at you. I know it feels like she is. Sometimes we make mistakes because that is what humans do. It's just like at preschool when someone doesn't share or hits a friend. Doing those things isn't okay, but we make the mistake because we aren't perfect, and not being perfect is okay. I think everyone does the best we can with the things we learned. Mom did the best she could, too, and she did make a mistake that hurt you. I'm sorry that happened. You deserve to feel loved and special because you are." I pause to take her hand, knowing she can only comprehend the depth of some of my words. "I want to go outside and dance more. Do you want to dance?"

"Will you pick me up and spin me?!" She sounds delightfully distracted from the conversation.

"Yeah! Maybe Mom will, also! Did you know she used to dance in college? She studied dance at two schools named Berkley and College of Alameda. She also practiced things called yoga and tai chi. I can talk to her and make sure she isn't mad and invite her to come with us."

"Mom is a dancer, too?! Wow! Maybe she can teach me some! Maybe she can teach me to spin lots without falling down!" I knew I could hook her with dance. I smile and nod in agreement as I pick her up, hug her tight, kiss her head carefully so I don't squish the lilac, and balance her on my hip.

She snuggles into the nook of my neck and shoulder, holding herself close across my body. I spin her around once to make her smile before we head through the living room.

We turn the corner past the television into our parents' room. Mom is lying on her side of the bed reading a book by James Michener, her favorite author. Her television is on, filling the silence with background noise. Perched across her nose are her bedtime glasses—the ones that are broken because she reads until she falls asleep at night and they get twisted and mangled when she rolls over.

"Stop," my four-year-old self whispers in my ear, "Do you see her? Remember how much she loves to read? She loves to read me that book that says *I love you forever, I like you for always, as long as I'm living my baby you'll be*."

"I remember that book," I whisper back to her. As we get closer, Mom starts to shrink and reverse into her younger self.

"Hey! What is she doing? She is getting small like me?" She asks without taking her eyes off Mom. We watch layers of age shed until Mom seems to be about four years old, also. Her book is now The Giving Tree and she is turning the pages really fast. Her eyebrows are moving dramatically as if she is anticipating an extreme plotline. I come to the edge of the bed and lean on the mattress before remembering it is a water bed and falling onto my back with Sierra on top of me and Mom's 4-year-old self's toes under us. We all start to giggle.

"Hi." Sierra sounds timid and plain.

"Hi! My name is Michelle. What is your name?" Mom surprises me with her direct sociality.

"I am Sierra. This is Sierra, too, and she is taking care of me. Are you done reading? Do you want to go outside and dance in the grass?" The child versions of us look at each other with the same huge chestnut eyes, the same shiny brown hair, and the same shy smile.

"Ok! I like to dance!" Michelle tosses her book aside and wriggles quickly out from underneath us, falling off the bed. I notice she is wearing patched jeans and a baseball t-shirt. I wonder if she inherited the outfit from her big brother. She skips out the door. We follow her back through the house, across the porch, and down the stairs onto the yard stage.

"Sierra, let me down!" Sierra tugs at my blanket cape, still unable to stop looking at Michelle, who is now practicing somersaults and cartwheels. I release her and she bounds and leaps over to Michelle. They begin to choreograph synchronized gymnastics; they hold hands and push-pull, embodying the magnetism and resistance of mothers and daughters. Michelle reaches above her head and spreads her fingers to show Sierra how to make a jazz frame. Sierra laughs and starts to mimic a lion's roar while she wiggles her fingers.

"I know something, too!" Sierra steadies her feet, "This is called a plié. I learned it in dance class. You reach down to the ground—you have to keep your back straight—then you move your arms like you are picking up a bunch of flowers, and you bring them back standing up and open your arms like you are giving the flowers to the people watching you! Try it!" Their heads are now bobbing up and down like buoys in Kachemak Bay as they start throwing imaginary flowers at an imaginary audience.

"Where did you get that crown?" Michelle asks.

"I made it!" Sierra responds enthusiastically, still bobbing.

“Oh,” Michelle stops bobbing and admires the lilacs. Sierra notices she has stopped and looks at her face.

“Have you ever seen a crown before? Did you ever make one?” From the inquisitive glint in her eyes, I know she is wondering what Michelle's life is like.

“No, I don't know how to make a crown. I only have brothers. I haven't been a queen before.” She looks bashful.

“Here, wear mine! It is really fun and it smells like flowers,” Sierra picks up her crown and sets it gently on Michelle's head, then moves her stray hair out of her eyes and tucks it behind her ear.

“You are now Queen Michelle the Beautiful! The important thing to know is that queens are always brave.” As their eyes meet, they mirror the same smile again, this time with a brilliant glow that radiates and amplifies between them. Suddenly Michelle starts to roll her body from side to side, head to toe, dancing in primal movements. She begins to grow back through her stages of life. Sierra takes a step back in awe, drops her jaw, and freezes, staring at Michelle. She is six now, doing happy feet and hopscotch. She is nine; demiplié, cambré, repeat, repeat. She is 15; chaine turn, kick ball change, grapevine. She is 22; glissade, plié, glissade, fan kick. She is 29; pique turn, pique turn, pique turn around Sierra as the 4-year-old follows in circles with her head. Michelle is 33; straight leg scorpion, barrel turn. She is 39; fouetté, battement, battement on the other leg, pirouette, pirouette, pirouette, and grand jeté over Sierra's head; gracefully landing while facing her, she makes eye contact, smiles tenderly, and curtsies into a sitting position on the grass. She is wearing a white sundress now and still has the crown upon her head. Sierra silently sprints toward Michelle, who has grown to the age of her mom. As her momentum collides with Mom's strong core, Mom holds her tightly in her arms and Sierra visibly collapses into her embrace.

"Mom, I thought you were mad at me," Sierra speaks in a weak voice through her tears.

"Oh, my daughter, my little flower fairy, I am not mad. I am scared, like you are," Mom melts with a heavy sigh into Sierra, curling over her body to protect her and kiss her head. "I never meant to hurt you. I'm sorry. I'm so sorry. I love you more than you can know right now." I approach them unnoticed and wrap my blanket cape around them just like Mom did when I was sick at night, placing my crown on Sierra's head, and watching them heal each other as the sunlight burns away their pain.

4

"Traumatized people chronically feel unsafe inside their bodies: The past is alive in the form of gnawing interior discomfort. Their bodies are constantly bombarded by visceral warning signs, and, in an attempt to control these processes, they often become expert at ignoring their gut feelings and in numbing awareness of what is played out inside. They learn to hide from their selves."
—Bessel A. Van der Kolk

"The attempt to escape pain is what creates more pain. [The question is] Not why the addiction but why the pain."
–Gabor Maté

Shortly after I told my family about my childhood, I felt the need to move my body a lot. I started jogging, which was something I loved in my teens. In the last spell of jogging regularly, I was training for a marathon that I never ran, because my doctor told me I could not possibly eat the amount of calories I needed for the run. That broke my heart. I listened to him and eventually quit running altogether, sinking into stagnance and depression.

I started smoking cigarettes. They made me feel dizzy and gave me an identity as a *smoker* to replace my identity as a *runner*. My health slowly declined over several years. The day after I graduated high school, I woke up nauseous. It seemed to come from nowhere and continued each morning. I would brush my teeth and dry heave until I felt stable enough to stand up.

Over the next six months, the stomach sickness turned into a series of kidney infections. I took pain killers and smoked pot to get through it. After several tests, one doctor told me there was nothing wrong with me except that I was an anxious person. I had never identified with the symptoms of anxiety and I felt dismissed and unimportant as I left her office.

When Western medicine didn't work, I saw a naturopath. He tested me for a candida yeast overgrowth, and I spent the next three months on a strict diet, taking supplements to strip my intestines of bacteria that sabotaged me. I found that self-sabotage is a learned behavior all the way down to a one-celled imprint in our gut. I lost a lot of weight. I was a size 2, the smallest I have ever been, and in one of the most unhealthy periods of my life.

Disarming the bacteria did not work for me. Over the following five years, I suffered through rashes, acid reflux, exhaustion, discomfort, and embarrassment from all these symptoms. I lived on emotions that controlled me, because I did not have the skills or health to regulate them. I was unable to remember things or think logically. Instead, I would react in snap decisions, yelling, saying things I later regretted, or staying silent as I used marijuana and television to numb my feelings. I felt so powerless over my health—over emotions that I didn't understand well enough to even look at—that I protected myself by numbing them. As I look back on it, I recognize that I felt as if I would die if I allowed myself to feel anything. The dysregulation felt like the buoy saving my life.

What I did not know then is that the only place we drown is in shallow water, wishing to experience the depth of who we are.

I was part of a failing medical system, seeing doctor after doctor and specialist after specialist, only to find out that nobody knew why I didn't feel well. They all had answers: that it was the bacteria, that I needed to see a nutritionist and eat differently, that I should sleep sitting upright, that I had a chemical imbalance, that I didn't methylate vitamins.

At 22, I was diagnosed with Polycystic Ovary Syndrome (PCOS). A year after an incorrectly-performed ultrasound, I was in the emergency room where a doctor who had PCOS herself caught the mistake and ordered another ultrasound. My now ex-boyfriend held my hand, and I felt my gaze blur as the voice of the technician echoed from far away, telling me that it may feel cold, that she would use gel, that we were almost done. It hurt to have the wand inserted, yet I was numb to the sensation. I sat frozen in the hospital chair, suddenly unable to breathe, holding back tears. I wanted to scream, I wanted to fight back what felt like an assault on my body, but I was no longer in it. I had escaped to survive, as I had learned from my childhood that you should not go into the bear's den to ask for shelter. When the bear's den was your own body, what choice did I have but to dissociate? I sat there, surviving until I could go home, get high, and forget the experience.

After battling the bacteria didn't change my symptoms, I started eating junk food. I would get high and eat fast food—anything cheap that I could microwave or cook easily—until I couldn't move, alternating between salty and sugary cravings. It was the only time I felt good. I got my fix of dopamine from marijuana and hits of serotonin from my food in order to stay alive. It kept me from forming new memories, which both prevented me from seeing any hope of a world without pain and rescued me from remembering the experiences of puking and dry heaving each morning, feeling raped by the ultrasound wand, or facing triggers from trying to create a loving relationship with another person. I had no time for anything but avoiding emotion and producing the chemicals that would keep me from killing myself.

Breakfast was smoking a bowl with a cup of coffee. Lunch was anything coated in bread or a starch fix to make it through the workday. After work, I smoked two more bowls to stop the pain in my stomach. Then I would go to class or finish my college homework before a dinnertime appetizer of more pot followed by the cycle of salt and sugar until I smoked again to fall asleep. Often, I would smoke in the middle of the night to sleep a few more hours before I woke up to purge again. This was the maintenance I needed to stay alive, yet it slowly killed me as I gained weight and lost myself.

It is easy for me to say I needed to do this because of all the pain I was in. Addicts are experts at rationalization. I knew it was not sustainable. While I believed food and marijuana was the only thing stopping my pain, I knew it was not healthy. While I avoided looking directly at it, I knew I was gaining weight, using more as my tolerance crept up and up, considering using different drugs, risking my job and my career as a teacher, and worst of all, risking making a terrible decision that harmed someone else while my judgment was clouded. Plenty of addicts do. I knew I was paying the price of real life experiences for numbness and isolation. I didn't have the resources to face what I avoided, so I stayed in the addiction and watched as my body, my relationships, and my work suffered. Like the most dangerous of addicts and those who experience mental health challenges, I performed well and was high-functioning, so it was easy to fly under the radar and convince myself I was in control while substances dictated my decisions. If anyone knew about my addiction, they did not mention it to me.

One day, I saw one of my sixth graders close his eyes and mouth inaudible words from across the room. I asked him later what he had been doing, and he explained, when he felt overwhelmed, he would shut his eyes and repeat that he was okay until he could feel his feet again, and then he would go on with the day. The strength of this boy inspired me. It was certainly a turning point for me, but it happened through beating myself up for allowing circumstances to control me while a 12-year-old was more capable than me to decide his destiny. I judged myself until I had to get in the ring and prove my own mind wrong.

I decided I would start using an affirmation each day. I thought I would start with something easy and say *I love you* in the mirror every morning. The first time I looked at my reflection without the distraction of brushing my hair or flossing my teeth, I realized I didn't recognize myself anymore. Who was that woman looking back at me? I learned the difference between easy and simple, and each time I started, I could get as far as *I lo—* before collapsing onto the bathroom floor, sobbing. I didn't believe it. I couldn't lie to myself and ignore the truth that I didn't love myself as an addict. The addiction was my costume, and to say those three words was to come head-to-head with the reality that if I loved myself, I wouldn't pump my body full of toxins, and I wouldn't have to numb myself just to survive. Words meant nothing when my actions screamed that I was not worthy of love. I could not tell my addict self the truth and keep the addiction, but I also could not lie to my own face.

I spent another year at odds with myself, trying to reconcile using with telling myself the truth. I used cocaine twice; both times, I spent the next day showering over and over as if I could scrub it off from the outside in. I wanted to use any drug someone would offer me, from advil to cough syrup to spice, which was newly legal to buy from smoke shops. I think I was lucky marijuana was my first drug of choice, and that I felt lazy and anti-social when I was high, because it may have stopped me from using more lethal substances. I never could make it through "I love you" during that time. "I love you" was not the truth. The truth was, I didn't want to stop using.

It wasn't until after I told my family the truth about my childhood that I reached pre-contemplation of recovery from addiction. I still didn't want to stop using. I couldn't imagine a life without dependence. I found that sobriety began not with wanting to stop using, but with *wanting to* want to stop. Telling my family the truth was enough of an act of love for myself that I was able to finally consider this.

My strongest coping skill is researching and intellectualizing what I don't understand to make it more comfortable. After I was diagnosed with PCOS I read books and blogs and watched videos through which I discovered that many women who have experienced sexual abuse get diagnosed with PCOS later on. They say there is no cure for it. Cysts cycle through growth on their own time, then release toxic fluid into the body in a painful burst. It feels like someone stabbing a syringe into my ovary, then pulsing for several seconds before the pain subsides. It stops me in my tracks and I can only focus on my breathing to get through it. Since it is a syndrome, if you surgically removed the cysts, they would grow back.

I changed my diet again, first cutting out dairy, then gluten. I was still smoking when I decided to start moving my body again. My new identity was held in the contrast of craving a cigarette after a 20-mile run, as if letting go of the cigarettes would mean I had to accept I was scared of unknown territory. I would only run before sunrise because I didn't want anyone to see me. I was ashamed of my body and how it jiggled when I ran. I have a gap in photos of myself for a span of several years because I wanted to erase any memory of it. The worlds of addiction and health started to merge, though I kept both hidden during the transition.

I found yoga and practiced regularly. I started going to a Kundalini class. The first time I went, I wept on the mat. When I left, my legs were trembling. Contrary to what we often believe, shaking muscles do not always indicate fatigue. My nervous system was so dysregulated that relaxation was a foreign territory. It is the combination of danger and emotion rushing through and from the body. Humans store our emotions in our connective tissues; without movement, massage, and other body-centered practices, we keep it there, creating disease. I had stored over two decades of trauma in my body at that point. I am still shaking it out today.

Though I had forced myself to forgo breakfast pot, I was still getting high in the evenings. I tried for a few weeks to stop altogether, but I went back to smoking every night. Every time it was available, I would use, and when I didn't have herb, I would smoke resin. I couldn't fall asleep without being high. Even when I did smoke, I would wake up in the night and lay awake for hours. This was a symptom of withdrawal. I decided to get rid of it so I had no choice.* I want to tell you this made it easier, but the truth is, I felt alienated because I was addicted to something people had said no one could get addicted to. "Marijuana isn't addictive" was the message I had received, and it made it nearly impossible to ask for help, because I was certain I would be laughed at and told to ask for help when I was addicted to a real drug.

I put all my pipes into a plastic bag with all the leftover resin and tucked it into a large sock that I placed on the driveway. I went into the garage and found a sledgehammer. This was all methodical and robotic for me, simply what had to be done to stop using. I heaved the hammer above my head and watched it slam down on the sock. As it hit the concrete and I heard the shatter of the glass, the emotions hit me. I screamed, tears flowing from my eyes as my body continued to swing the hammer over and over until I collapsed in exhaustion.

Immediately, I went back to numbing myself. My body could only take so much emotion before it went into autopilot to survive again. I sat in the driveway atop the thin layer of crusty snow and stared at the sock as if my lover were telling me I betrayed them. I opened it. Inside was a sticky tar mixed with glass dust. I wanted to puke at the smell of addiction.

I would do this ritual again two months later. Then again, two years later. Then a couple more times over the following 8 years. Each time I went through the cycle, it took less time for my self-control to dissolve and less time to quit again. In that moment, though, I felt the fear that led to moments of great courage later on.

After a month of sober jogging and kundalini yoga, I decided to join a training facility. I emailed the owner before I signed up, admitting how scared I was. She told me simply to show up. I showed up. For the first three months, I felt anxious every time I went, cried in my car before driving there, and kept the feelings of disgust about my body and my weakness to myself. Regardless of my feelings, I kept showing up.

During the same period of time, I finally showed up for counseling. I had planned it for six months and I had tried it five years before, but I hadn't been ready. I never took it seriously and I wasn't ready to unpack my trauma, so it didn't help me. I started looking at my trauma and shaking through exercise. I cycled this way intensely for two years: unpack trauma and shake, unpack trauma and shake, over and over. I started dancing at Zumba and playing volleyball again. I ran more often and for further distances. I kept training, lifting heavier weights.

On April 10, 2014, I took a personal day to celebrate the one year anniversary of the day I started running again. I planned to run 10 miles; the longest run I had accomplished that year. After 2 miles, I decided I would do 13 for a half-marathon, just a little further than I had planned. After 8 miles, I was set on running the full marathon. In the middle of the longest run I had done in six years, I decided to make it the longest of my life. I mapped what I knew to be at least 26 miles in my head and just kept running. When I finished, I drove my course to find it was a 29-mile run. I said to myself in my driveway, “Well, now I know I can do that.” I walked inside and washed my dishes before smoking a cigarette.

In 20 months, I had done over 100 hours of Zumba, 350 hours of yoga, 10 mornings of swimming, almost 400 hours of training with weights, and almost 1,800 miles of running. That's almost 1,100 hours of exercise in about 615 days. This is how much my body needed in order to complete the cycle of feel-and-shake at the beginning of my recovery.

I held on to cigarettes until the end of that time. I had lost 100 pounds and thought I would gain it back if I quit. I was still an addict, but now they were the socially acceptable forms of addiction that diet and exercise provide. I became obsessed with my body's fat content and the inches around my waist. I threw away my cigarettes because I knew I could run faster if I didn’t smoke. Three months later, I threw away my scale as soon as I completed the weight loss. I took 30 minutes off my third marathon immediately after that.

I have been every size between 2 and 20, and I have noticed patterns in how I am treated at each size. I know very well what thin privilege is, and I recognize it when I experience it. Virgie Tovar said, “When people say they want to lose weight, they often mean 'I want to be respected. I want to be loved. I want to be seen. I want liberation from fear and self-loathing.' Weight loss culture will never give us those things because it is founded on fear/hate-based systems like sexism, racism, classism and ableism.” I felt this deeply during this time. I recognized its similarity to the feeling of being loved in abuse. I felt cared for because of what my body did or how it was controlled. I longed for someone to ask me about my recovery plan instead of my exercise plan.

As humans, we often follow the comforting things at the end of each other's stories. We want to know how it feels to have lost weight, to be healthy, or to have movement, but we don't ask how it felt to get there or what led us to make such a drastic change. We replace the truth that is the anger of the sledgehammer, the anxiety of the cigarette smoke, and the numbness of all emotion with the facts of protocol. We ask, "What is your step-by-step plan to get thin?" What I hear beneath it is, "What will it take for me to feel fulfilled?"

To this I reply: go look in the mirror and see yourself, perhaps for the first time, and say, "I am here to keep you safe and show you love."

Then, stop running from yourself.

*Note: A lot of people use substances which are dangerous to quit without tapering off. If I were quitting alcohol or opioids, I would have had to go to a facility to make sure quitting wasn't fatal for me.

5

"You were sick, but now you're well again, and there's work to do."
—Kurt Vonnegut

"If you desire healing,
let yourself fall ill
let yourself fall ill."
—Rumi

"Soon, when all is well, you're going to look back on this period of your life and be so glad that you never gave up."
—Brittany Burgunder

I think it is abnormal to know the exact moment we fully recover from adversity. It's hard to tell the difference between specific trauma and the human condition, and interesting how our physical bodies react to our mental, emotional, and spiritual health. This was how it happened for me.

For two months, I had episodes of sudden, sharp pain in my womb. I would fold over and breathe heavily until it passed. The pain felt like a creature that was black and sticky like tar, oozing up from the deepest parts of me, reaching to strangle me from the inside. When the pain would come, it would squeeze my organs and muscle fibers to debilitate me. It came from me, but it was not of me. During that time, I also had strange visions. I did not see them as hallucinations but as flashes of scenes witnessed by my mind's eye. They started with people I did not know: prisoners of war, clowns from horror movies, or dirty coal miners coughing to their deaths, all reaching to me for help. The images didn't feel scary, though it seemed their purpose was to frighten me. After several weeks, the visions changed into child versions of myself. In black and white, I would see her bleeding out her eyes or sleeping in a crib as blood slowly dripped down the walls around her.

Owls started showing up on the porch and hooting at me every night. I dreamt of them in threes. I would go to coffee shops and see owl paintings on the walls as if they were following me everywhere. I felt the message that I needed to give birth to something to transition into a new season of life.

The only way I knew how to deliver something that was calling me from my subconscious was to follow the imagery. I had used this skill before to tap into an altered conscious state and get the intuitive information I wanted. Usually it was related to what I was doing in the physical world, but this time, it seemed spiritual warfare was calling me into my mind.

I had a sense that this womb creature had been within me my whole life. It was woven into me and I feared what would happen if it wasn't filling that space. What would move into my body then? Would I change? As I realized I could choose what to fill the space with, the fear started to dissipate.

The visions continued, but I pressed into them and talked to the people who came to me. They asked me to release them. I did not know how to do that, but I listened to their stories and awarded a universal forgiveness. I believed they would do differently next time, and I stayed with them. I heard stories of war and murder. I imagined being so scared that all I could do is project that fear into those around me. Of course we choose the most vulnerable ones; the children, the victims, the insecure. If we can be the ones causing fear, we no longer feel fearful. Sometimes we believe this is the only way out, and I get that. I lived that.

When I was nine years old, I bullied a classmate at school. She was a new girl whose family moved around often. She invited me and my friends to play outside. We agreed, but instead we said mean things to her passively, so that when she told us we were being mean, we could defend ourselves by saying it was a joke or that she didn't understand what we meant. This is how people manipulate others and abuse them; by gaslighting them. If I can be cruel and then tell you you're crazy, I have all the power.

On the swingset, we teased her for matching our pace, saying she must be a lesbian if she wanted to be that close to girls. For kids on our playground, that was called 'being in our cookie jar,' to which we quickly added sexual overtone. The girl started crying and ran away. I questioned what I was doing for a fleeting moment, but I quickly rationalized my behavior with the belief that refusing to participate would cost me my friends. 'If I am scared, I get to protect myself and take back my power by harming another.' I did not think of it this directly as a child, of course, but this is what I was doing.

Like wolves hunting prey, we positioned ourselves so she ran straight for more of us on the hill. We felt powerful as we closed in to circle around her and started chanting, "Get out of my cookie jar, get out of my cookie jar…"

We took turns asking her questions: "Is this why you had to switch schools, because you couldn't stop getting in girls' cookie jars?"

"Is this why you wouldn't stop staring at me in the locker room during swim lessons last week?"

"How many girls have you kissed on the bus after school?" All of these questions came rapid-fire while the background chanting continued. We were vicious, showing all of our fangs, and she hid her head in her hands as if she could play dead and our pack would lose interest. What choice did she have?

Finally the whistle blew. We ran away, shoulders back, chins up, as if we ran the world, or at least the world of the playground behind the school. We were untouchable. We could do anything and get away with it.

This girl was brave and, in the end, much stronger than any of us. She told our teacher what had happened and we all ended up having a conversation before we went home. I remember when, in the middle of this meeting, the empathy hit me. The terror from being circled by other girls and chanted at would have haunted me for months. I proudly played a role in torturing that girl. I started to cry in disappointment with myself and the feelings I imagined she had.

I apologized to her. I think we all apologized to her. I felt shameful for several months after that, which was a fair consequence for what I had done. I tried to talk to her more after that day. I would ask her how she was in the mornings and invite her to sit with me at lunch. She never accepted my invitations. She never wanted to talk to me after that. I had betrayed her and she was not willing to forgive me or allow me to earn back her trust.

She moved away the summer after that year, and I never saw her again. I still wonder what happened to her and how she is doing today. I deserved losing the privilege of knowing. It was painful.

Because of this incident, I related to the visions that were coming to me. I knew the monsters were scared. The only reason we have for being monsters is to protect ourselves by outweighing our fear with power over others. When I remembered this, I went deep into my imagination.

I knew I was undertaking something that would change my life. I don't know how the spirit world works, or if there are other dimensions, or how our energy bodies change our journeys, but I know from my experience that spiritual birth is powerful. I spoke to my womb each night in the shower to ask what I should know and tell it I was all in. I made a painting with my own blood to allow my expression to release into the world. What happened that day is the most powerful voyage I have embarked on. Perhaps it would be considered a pilgrimage to recovery.

I surrendered to the visualization. I had my warrior outfit on, the one I had imagined so many times when I needed to harness bravery. I arrived at a vacant penitentiary. Barbed wire spiraled atop a brick wall with an open rusty door. I walked into the building and down the stairs, entering the first cell. There sat a man in an electric chair. He looked at me woefully as I unstrapped him. He nodded in repentant gratitude and drifted down the hall the way I had come.

I continued the opposite way, stepping around puddles on the floor and avoiding the beads of water dripping from the ceiling. There was moss overgrowth and black mold emerging from the corners. The end of the corridor revealed another open cell. Inside towered a throne with sharp triangular spikes pointing upwards from the back of the chair. Ralph waited on it, rewarding my entrance with empty black eyes as if he were possessed. Beside him sat a small canister of gasoline and a matchbook. Without hesitation, I poured the fuel around the throne, stepped into the doorway, lit a match, and threw it in. He did not try to stop me, but energetically sanctioned what I was doing. The room collapsed, the throne dissolved into a pile of ash, and out of the small mushroom cloud walked a young boy. I knew this was Ralph. Without hesitation, he extended his hand for me to hold.

"They said you would release me," he said, smiling at me through tired eyes.

"I don't know how to do that. Did they say how?"

"No. I just know I want to go home first." I took his hand, soft and small, and embraced the fearful determination to return to his childhood home. As we stepped back into the hallway, the prison transformed into rural Canada. There was a small decaying brick-red farmhouse with a front porch rotting at the floorboards. We walked inside and found it lifeless, the furniture dusty and falling apart as if it had been abandoned. In the back room, we found two cans of gasoline and another matchbook. Small Ralph nodded at me and we began lining the perimeter of each room. He threw in the lit match from his place on the porch and we stood in the yard together, watching the house burn to the ground.

"This is all I needed," he whispered as the fire lit his eyes until all we could see was the black scorch mark in the shape of the foundation. "They can't come back now." I smiled at him because I could feel his relief, but I did not know the specifics of what he was describing.

Our next stop was a massive graveyard. There were hundreds of headstones arranged in rows forming a perfect square. I stood before the grave centered in the first row of stones. Grayscale bodies of children emerged from the earth. They were dressed in torn clothing, some bruised or bloodied, and each of them stared at me in anticipation. I studied them all, empathizing with their sorrow and bewilderment, and sensing their hope at seeing me with them. As I wondered how I would fulfill their expectations, they ascended towards the sky as if the rapture had begun. Before they reached the clouds, they stopped to beckon me. I looked to Boy Ralph for direction and he stared at me, expressionless. At that moment, from the grave in front of me rose a 7-year-old version of myself. She wore a full-sleeve white nightgown that had been tattered and stained. Her eyes met mine with a smile and I noticed they had quit bleeding since my previous visions. She was confident. She reached out her hand to Boy Ralph. They both looked at me and nodded, then drifted skyward together. The clouds opened up and they joined hands, taking their places in front of the children. I felt impressed, as I have many times before, by how certain my little-girl-self was in her mission and service.

I turned around and found myself in front of a magnificent spruce forest. The air here was crisp and light, inviting me into its song. It broke by a trail that I followed, crunching needles under my boots and listening to the melodies in the air. My gaze was drawn upwards as if to ask, w*hy me?* My feet hit grass as I entered a wide clearing where a dozen women sat in a circle around a fire. They all wore layers of black clothing embellished with natural elements such as moss hats, twig broaches, leaf and flower crowns, budding earrings, and bark leggings. All were barefoot and some had decorated their faces with mud designs. They were chanting and playing drums.

I completed the circle by sitting on the empty stump. They ended their song and my grandmother, who I never met in real life, announced cheerfully, “We have been waiting for you!” All the women agreed with enthusiastic nods and eager smiles.

“I have been here for centuries, Dearie,” the eldest of them exclaimed as she brushed a piece of moss from her hat off her eyelid. It appeared to have been growing for so long I couldn't tell where her hair ended and the moss began. “Look! I have grown some old man's beard behind my ear!” They all laughed as if they were straight out of a Mary Poppins story set in the wilderness.

“Here, have a drum,” said a younger woman I did not recognize as she handed me a large ceremonial drum and beater. “Your role in our family is to keep the heartbeat. Just bang a steady beat so we can tell you what we have to say.” I started with a slow pace as I studied the faces around me. Some were ancestors I remembered; others, I had never seen.

“I am here to tell you we are sorry,” said one of them. “We have not been honest and that wasn't fair to you. We have been building this circle for you.”

“I am here to let you know we have been holding you the whole time,” said another. “You have come in and out of this circle dozens of times; each time, we wiped your memory so you could be fully human. We know there have been times you felt alone, but we have always been present.”

“I need to say you are brave,” the eldest had a soft tone

now. “You are the only one who stood up at council and said you could do this. You move the Earth with your steps; you recharge by standing against the wind. Your soul burns ferocious as fire and your courage raises the tides of the ocean. I know you are feeling inadequate to accept this power, but I agreed when you stood up long ago that I would retire and become the voice in stillness that speaks to you. There are times you have wanted to run away—and every one of us would have—but you did not. This is why you are the one who will continue this process. You can do it, you are doing it, and you will continue as long as your heart is open.”

“Finally,” my great-grandmother Nan said as she revealed a tiny jar of jam in her hand, a symbol for me to confirm it was her, “the only commitment you remain responsible for is the one you made to yourself. Your family may yearn to be saved, but this is not the contract you agreed to. You simply stay committed to yourself and they will choose to follow in their own time. Let them have their own time.”

The circle of women stared at me in solace. They all whispered in unison, “Our heartbeat has returned. We are ready to give our power to her. We recognize this not as sacrifice of self, but as contribution to raise us all into rejoiced oneness. She has dedicated herself to join our circle and, in turn, we dedicate our support now. Release us, release us, release us...”

As they chanted, a gust of wind hit my back and the beat of the drum seemed to move through my hand faster and faster until the sound burst from our collective chests. Pulled by our hearts, we raised up to the tops of the trees surrounding us and their black clothes were shed and fell to the ground. Underneath were layers of white lace, silk, and linen. Their hair turned gray, wrinkles appeared as their eyes closed, and one by one, their faces began to shine with the smile of a peaceful death.

Before I could smile back, I plummeted down to the earth and crashed hard in the heart of a cave. I lifted myself off the wet cobblestone. In front of me I could see a long corridor lit by candles and smelling of petrichor. The sounds of dripping water and the echo of my boots were all I heard. In this moment I finally felt the fear. Not only was I having a vividly theatrical experience, but it had brought me into the unexplored darkness. I came to the end of the hall and could only turn left, where I saw an old man sitting on a throne. He was wearing a robe that was infested with mold and a matching cape lined with lichen. His skin was weathered and splotched with moles and skin tags. Atop his head was a shining crown that matched the rings on his fingers.

I met his eyes, which were a piercing bright blue. I gazed at his drooping cheeks and a smirk that suggested he had been waiting to prove his power to me.

On instinct, I stood up taller, as if bracing myself. The energy conveyed to me that this was Ralph's father, my great-grandfather. Though I only knew him from stories and had never seen him, I later discovered that he looked exactly like he did in this vision. Thus far, my job had been to release the people I had come across, so I continued to do so. I took a deep breath and screamed at him as loud as I could.

He looked at me and bellowed, "You are no match for me, little girl." He followed with a sinister cackle. I felt every desperate moment of helplessness I had growing up, every look of despair that each character had shown me on their face in the weeks leading up to this moment, and most potently, the faraway stare on my grandfather's face when he told me years ago that he never had a father.

I took a deep breath and screamed again, this time with specks of my saliva catching the candle light on their way to him. I watched his clothes fall to the floor and the skin peel off his bones, turning him into a skeleton with blue eyes staring at me. I noticed a flash of fear in them and took advantage of it.

One more time, I screamed, and a gust of wind from the space behind me united with my voice, reducing his bones to dust that swirled into the darkness. His crown clattered to the seat of the throne before a rumbling from the left swallowed me in a current that yanked me out of the cave. I tumbled around, engulfed in water and reaching for anything to hold on to. Everything went black.

I woke up in a puddle. I felt heavy and soaked. Opening my eyes, I saw it was not water, but blood I sat in. My armor was gone and I was wearing a long white dress that had been stained. My lungs filled easily with pure, weightless air. A light shone in my eyes from above, and I saw the image of a European Jesus, the kind you would recognize from a Sacred Heart candle in a tall glass jar. I closed my eyes. This couldn't be right. I was not raised with any religious teachings, and if I had been, I would believe in some sort of 5-armed Hindu hippie god, right? She would at least be a woman. I opened them again, and the same Jesus stood above me. I closed my eyes for a second time.

"Stop trying to make me something I'm not," Jesus laughed.

"Okay!" I was surprised. "I just thought I would be rebirthed by a woman, I guess."

"You birthed yourself, Sierra." He continued, "You are free. You healed it all and you can go help other people now. Move forward. It is done."

I stood up and absorbed these words. I healed myself. I birthed myself. I did it. I did it! I was jumping up and down and dancing and hugging Jesus, celebrating the way a football player would after scoring a touchdown.

"I did it." I looked Jesus in the eyes. "They said I couldn't do it, but I did. It's done."

"You are faithful, Sierra," Jesus replied. "Don't forget why you chose this path. You are free now, and you know what comes next. Keep your faith."

With this, he disappeared into the soft white image in my mind. I tried to follow him but instead landed on a tree branch high above my favorite place, a bluff overlooking the Fox River Flatts in Alaska. Below me, there was a forest opening to a field of long grass. I was in a nest I had made of eagle feathers and cotton seeds. The sun was low on the horizon, preparing to set, and I noticed some small yellow lights in the field below. They were shaped like cookie-cutter humans, playing and dancing. When they touched each other, their light got brighter. As the sunlight began to fade, I noticed other cookie-cutter humans that were dark. They were running around in a chaotic pattern. When they touched the lights, the lights dimmed. I watched curiously as these humans of light and darkness interacted in pain and pleasure together. Three owls landed on the branch next to me. They looked at me, then at the human condition below. If releasing hearts was my purpose, I decided, I would absolutely show up. But first, I closed my eyes to rest.

6

"You cannot kill a monster
until you are willing to see it in the mirror.
Until you recognize its shape in your own skin."
-Dylan Garity

I have never been anywhere like Alaska. It is heaven for the people who love it. The motto there is, "North to the Future." Though gold was what brought people to Alaska, it abounds in other resources: five types of salmon, halibut, cod, crab, shrimp, scallops; grizzly bears, brown bears, black bears, polar bears; caribou, moose; eight species of whale; at least a dozen species of edible berries, over 15 kinds of edible mushrooms; and glacier water. Those are just the resources that provide nutrition. There are also 129 million acres of forests, coal, natural gas, over 17 billion barrels of oil, and over 470 species of birds, including the Bald Eagle. Alaska is the largest state in the nation and is known for everything being oversized, from animals to mountains to oceans to vegetables, with records of 138-pound cabbages and a 2,051-pound pumpkin.

I don't know what it's like not to be Alaskan, but what people have noticed about me is that I decide what I want to do and I do it. I decide how I want to be and I learn how to be that. I have been nicknamed The Queen of Slay. This was not because I ran marathons or started a business or published my first book. I was given this nickname because I was the first woman this person had heard speaking openly about being suicidal. She said I was living well because I was honest, brave, and relatable. Alaskans are authentic that way. We are pioneers. If we want a job that doesn't exist, we start a business; we learn to chop wood, fix our cars, and be patient when a moose lays down in the road after we honk at them. We exercise the same patience when we put snowsuits on our children for 6 months out of the year. Alaskans perform and create throughout our lives, seeking education that includes the arts.

Alaska is changing with time. The sea ice has melted, there is less oil production, seismic testing is being done in the waters, and the Article National Wildlife Refuge is being targeted to find more oil. Pebble Mine is pushing to open for coal production. Wildfires increase while the summer rain decreases and temperatures break records. Some resources are depleting due to climate change and overfishing. Clams are rarely available for harvest and red tide is spreading. I was born in 1987, which was arguably the height of Alaska's available resources. As a small child, I regularly ate king crab for dinner, dug for razor clams with my hands, and drank milk from the local creamery. I knew the names of every person who lived on my road.

In 1989, almost 2 million barrels of oil were produced per day, and over 675 million pounds of salmon were caught that season. I was turning two years old. We lived in the town of Homer, known for halibut fishing at the end of the road on Kachemak Bay. Alaska was thriving in resources, yet still went into a recession. The job market was declining, the real estate market crashed, and on March 24th, an oil tanker owned by Exxon struck a reef in Prince William Sound, spilling an estimated 11 million gallons of crude oil onto the coastline and into the waters. The repercussions of these events would take several books to describe in full. In my story, this meant that our house and income was threatened. My dad worked in commercial fisheries year-round while my mom cared for me and my brother. My parents chose to sell their home and move to Anchorage for a year. We moved into a house across the street from my grandparents.

My grandpa Ralph and grandma Kay were from Canada. Ralph moved to Alaska in 1954 to pursue a career in retail paint and Kay married and joined him in 1955. I discovered in the Christmas of 2010 that our family knew very little about Ralph. We were playing a game I had created that involved writing personal facts onto slips of paper and trying to guess which fact belonged to whom. Each time I read one of Ralph's, it took a long time for someone to guess it was his.

In 2014, Ralph called me to apologize for hurting me. It was not the first time he apologized, but it was the first time he started the conversation. Because I am passionate about studying behavior and I truly care about people, I was able to put my pain aside to ask, "How did you get to the point of choosing this?" I saw him as someone who deserved to be known, and I believed I could learn from him.

I wanted to know what path led him to pedophilia. I asked if I could visit to talk with him about his life. From my childhood, I had learned manipulation; I knew how to get what I wanted. I appealed to his narcissism, making it about him so that he agreed. I also knew I would never get an answer as to why he abused me—because he didn't know—and that, no matter how much I wanted to, I would never be able to save him; he had to do that himself.

The next weekend, we spent over 4 hours sitting together

in his living room. I secretly set up my phone to video tape him speaking. I hoped to capture evidence of a grandfather on my video screen that I could go back to when it hurt and remember he was a human, even though I knew I could not be attached to an outcome. After I left, I would learn that the microphone was broken and I didn't record any of his voice on the video.

Ralph grew up the oldest of three children, two boys and one girl, in New Westminster, British Columbia. He described his childhood with little emotion. His father, Stuart, worked long hours and did not own a car. His mother, Gladys, spent a lot of time raising her children on her own. Ralph told me that his dad would often come home only on the weekends. His mom spent a lot of time in the hospital, first with polio and then breast cancer. He described his childhood as "watching my mom die while I took care of my brother and sister." Even when saying these words, he seemed to feel nothing, though I could see distress in his eyes, which avoided mine as he spoke. He recited his past as if it was a news report, facts without feelings. Ralph could never tell the truth for this reason; the truth contains the 'what' of events and the 'how' of emotions we feel, and when we leave out either one, we aren't authentic; we are safely hiding from the risk of vulnerability.

He claimed that he did not like children very much, and I believe this is a product of never getting to be one himself. Children aren't as fun to be around if we can't relate to them from our own experiences. He did admit that he didn't like this situation, and I could tell he still held a lot of resentment for his father. Ralph told me his dad did not impact him, saying, "How could my dad have had an influence on my life? I never had a dad, so it doesn't affect my life," continuing to tell half the truth.

I have heard both Ralph and my dad say, “My father wasn't present in my life.” Comparatively, Ralph was much more present than his own father. That's the power of seeing a bigger picture and hearing someone's story—we begin to understand their behavior. Ralph's father wasn't physically present, so he felt confident in his own fatherhood because he was. My dad wished for an emotional presence, to be told he was loved, to be nurtured and validated. Ralph never fully understood these needs, but he did better than his own father based on what he knew. Sadly, sometimes our best is not good enough. We repeat the cycles we see without realizing there are other options. We don't ask about the things we don't know about. There is no excuse, and placing blame doesn't help, so we pass pain on to the people we love. No matter who we are, no matter where we come from, we all do it, simply because no one is perfect.

When Ralph was six, he traveled to visit his family in California. He was in the backseat of the car when he fell and hit his head on the pavement, splitting it open. They did not go to the hospital, so he never got stitches. I could feel the bump on the back of his skull. I wondered how it affected his brain. I wondered how it affected his emotional wellbeing.

He started working when he was 14, digging dirt, repairing roofs, and taking on odd jobs at houses nearby. His younger brother taught him how to drive a tractor a couple years later. He would give his money to his mom to help pay bills while she was sick. He went to high school, which was optional in his time, and graduated with focuses in welding and carpentry. He was denied from joining the Canadian Navy because of his poor eyesight. His younger brother was accepted, and he was jealous. Ralph went to the American Navy to ask permission to join, which was allowed since he had been denied by Canada. They gave him permission to enter The Merchant Marines, and he went to training to become a crewmember, then a supervisor of freight—just below the captain and second mate. He did this for several years and traveled all over the world. As he told me about this time of his life, he showed me the faded, blurry tattoos on his arms that served as visual memories.

He had all kinds of stories about traveling the world as a Marine. He bought cigarettes that were cheap in other countries and traded them for more expensive items when he got home. He birthed calves to heffers in the holds of the ship when a storm slowed their schedule at sea. He went to brothels with his shipmates who paid women for sex. He claimed to be disgusted by this. I doubted his response and want to say he joined in; however, I can only recognize this as bias—I do not know whether his sex addiction started then or developed later on. He delivered to the Philippines, Africa, England, The United States, Venezuela, Argentina, New Zealand, and Australia in the five years he was enlisted.

Ralph loved to travel and would continue to take cruises throughout his life. I recalled the small motorhome he maintained during my childhood. He would buy cheesy t-shirts that read, "Someone that loves me went to Canada and all I got was this t-shirt," and "I ♥ The Caribbean," and he would show us photos from his trips when he returned. This was back when you had to develop rolls of film, and there would be hundreds of photos all over the table. Most of them were photos of plants and flowers, and the rest were posed pictures of him and my grandmother, sometimes with parrots on their shoulders.

When Ralph returned to Canada after the Merchant Marines, he worked in a whiskey distillery. This is where he met my grandmother. On their first date, he asked her to a concert where they danced. I remembered that they would dance together sometimes, when I was younger.

Ralph's uncle managed a California paint chain that needed a manager in Alaska. He offered Ralph the job and he and Kay decided they would marry and move to Alaska. He told stories of going dancing at the bars when they arrived. He had lots of bar stories, drinking stories, lake stories, camping stories, and stories of walking around downtown Anchorage when there were fewer people and more dirt roads. They both became American citizens in Alaska.

Ralph worked in the paint department at Allen and Peterson until 1989 while Kay raised the kids. It was Kay who coached her kids' teams and led the girl scouts. She put love into action the way Ralph never could and continued to show compassion to the disadvantaged for as long as she lived.

The garden at their Anchorage home was always immaculate. Ralph loved to grow flowers, vegetables, and berries on all sides of the house. In the windows bloomed African violets in every shade of purple and pink.

As Ralph talked, he hinted at the truth without speaking it directly. This relieved him of any responsibility and freed him from emotionally connecting with his memories. When I asked him if he had ever cheated on his wife, he said no, but he told me about the neighbor who used to have a huge fish tank in her home across the street. I later learned he had written a love letter to her in an attempt to have an affair, but she returned it to my grandmother. I don't know whether he ever had an affair with someone, but he certainly tried. While we talked, it was as if he wanted to tell me the truth, but he was so programmed to rationalize his behavior and stifle his feelings that he could not say it aloud. It was almost as if there were a part of him that wanted the truth to come out, so he would give me just enough information to piece it together.

I asked him if he had ever touched another child. He said no and did not follow this answer with a vague story. In the research we have about pedophiles, it's almost unheard of that someone would have only one victim. A pedophile has a sexual attraction to children. I do not know whether Ralph experienced that or if he was a sex addict for whom I was a convenient target.

Ralph primarily used alcohol and sex to numb his emotions. He had done this for so long that he sometimes had a sexual response to stress. My family has shared stories with me of Ralph getting an erection during high-stress situations. Like with any addiction, our bodies crave the chemical more and more over time, asking to be "fixed" through anxiety, sweating, shaking, and other methods. When the chemical answer comes from sex, the physiological method becomes erectile.

Researchers used to believe that a person who had been abused in their childhood was likely to abuse children in adulthood. More accurately, any childhood chaos often leads to chaos in adulthood, whether addiction, abuse, codependence, depression, or other mental illness. Humans learn by observing behavior, and we tend to mimic the things we see. Those of us who endured abuse in our childhood have much higher rates of mental illness and physical disease, and even a shorter life expectancy. We cannot know exactly how these risks will present themselves in each of us, and it isn't helpful to try.

I asked Ralph if he had ever been molested or seen another child molested. He said no, but this time, he had another vague follow-up story. He told me that, at some point in his childhood, his family had a boy come to live with them. The boy's family wasn't able to take care of him, so he lived with Ralph and his family for a while. The look on his face when he told me this was distant and perplexed. I don't have enough context to know how this story is related to Ralph's experience with molestation in childhood, but I trust the pattern to reveal that there was an incident he had decided not to feel and could never speak of directly.

Ralph acknowledged specific instances of abusing me. When I brought up my memories, he would tell me he remembered some of them and say he didn't know why he did it. Once in a while, he would mention how my body responded, as if he was trying to make sense of it or wondering if I'd wanted it. Our bodies can respond physiologically against our will, which must not be misunderstood as consent. Sometimes my body would do that, and it was confusing. As an adult, it has been a tangled mess of emotions, bodily functions, and triggers that connect everything together to confuse the meanings of love, sex, desire, and choice.

Ralph could not remember everything that I did, nor did he understand the intense and lasting impact this experience had on me. He never questioned why I felt the way I did as an adult; he never told me I was wrong, and he always showed up when I asked him to talk about it. I was able to get something from my abuser that so many survivors lack—space to process without pushback. Had I not set strong boundaries and followed through on them, had I chosen to keep hiding secrets, had I asked permission to believe and process my experiences, this would not have happened. I did the work necessary to come to this space, and I took the time alone to rage, to scream, to cry, to fall apart, and to be vulnerable in ways I would not allow Ralph to see. He could not hide from me or these stories. It was perhaps the only time in his life that someone was holding him accountable by asking him to talk about the truth; a truth he could not change because I was there to experience it myself. It may have been the only time in his life when someone knew how selfish, how cruel, and how deeply dysfunctional he was, yet chose to come back and speak to him with respect that many thought he didn't deserve.

I didn't go to him that day out of compassion or pity or in search of a happy ending to mitigate the pain I was feeling. I went out of my own fascination with behavior. I went out of concern that he could be abusing another child. I went because I didn't want him to get away with this and because I wanted to psychoanalyze him and finally stop taking personally any of the abuse I had been through. Make no mistake—I did not go there for Ralph but for fear of others' wellbeing and for my self-serving reasons.

I asked if he had ever considered getting help with his addiction to sex. He replied, “What sex addiction? I don't have a problem with sex.” Ralph was never able to openly admit that he had any addiction, despite knowing he had hurt his family deeply. He apologized to me three different times for what he had done and openly talked about how his children hated him.

This was true in part, but it seemed he said it to solicit pity for the attention he never got in his childhood. He believed the person he had hurt the worst in his life was my dad. He said he had treated his oldest son worse than his father treated him. The only ways he knew to show love were promising money in his will or writing letters. At this point, he had written so many letters to convince women to sleep with him that they didn't hold any value. Ralph didn't have the skills to repair relationships, and he didn't speak any love languages besides giving emotionless material gifts.

If he were to change something about his life, he would have never left the Merchant Marines. Like many people, Ralph had difficulty loving others and accepting they could love him. While he could barely articulate it, I believe he understood the impact our relationships had on each other, and he was ashamed of the consistency and the depth with which he had hurt his family over decades. Yet, he seemed desperate that I would find fulfillment through what he failed at: he told me my life would be improved by getting married and having children.

When I left that day, I looked at the house across the street where we had lived in 1989. I knew this was where the abuse had started, though I had only one vague memory of it. I was standing in the kitchen wearing a blue jumper. I could see the refrigerator, the tile floor, and the light above me. All I knew was something abnormal had just happened. All I have is this flash of a memory.

Like many survivors of abuse, I didn't trust myself that this was true; instead, I gaslighted my own experience. Many years later, I asked my mom what the kitchen in that house looked like. Sure enough, the details of the room matched my memory, giving me permission to believe myself. I now have a much clearer memory of events and emotions from my childhood than many people I've met.

When I was a child, I had the strong sense that there were things I couldn't see around me. I felt like I was surrounded by energy everywhere I went. This was not weird to me; nobody had told me it should be weird. I believed I was not alone and therefore felt more protected. Whether that was something I needed for survival or a type of sixth sense doesn't matter.

I was not raised with any kind of spirituality or religious understanding. My parents read me the Children's Bible and I had a vague idea what prayer was, but I talked to the universe long before I knew there was a specific way people engaged in that dialogue. When I was a little older, I let Jehovah's Witnesses into my home because I enjoyed the stories they told me. Of course, I was not given permission to do this, and I was quickly ordered to stop letting strangers in the house.

In the second grade, I watched two of my classmates fight over glue. One of them was doing something particularly annoying and messy to the other. At that moment, pragmatically and silently, I declared to myself that my peer had not had as many lives as me and therefore did not learn the lesson about annoying others with glue yet. In that moment, I decided I would have patience with others because they would learn all the lessons in time. Besides, though I had lived many lives, I may not have learned all the lessons, either. As I recall, this was the first time I adopted an internal dogma. I knew God was all around me, so I had less interest in defining God than in asking for guidance or having tea parties in the forest with them.

I relied heavily on my spirituality to feel connected with my family. I decided Ralph's annoying behaviors were his lessons to learn and experiencing them were mine. I believed I somehow chose those experiences before my life began so I could evolve, and while they led to a choice no child should have to make—to save her family from pain by staying silent about her abuse—they also allowed me to see myself in Ralph twenty years later. When I left his house and saw the house across the street where my life was changed forever, I learned something I didn't go there to learn: though Ralph and I would soon be very different, at the beginning of this journey, we were the same. He had wanted to save his family. He had lost his childhood by caring for something that a child should not care for. He felt disconnected, unseen, and invalidated by his family. He had spent decades keeping unprocessed secrets and used substances and power dynamics to survive. He had internalized his feelings, lashed out at his family, and avoided emotions. The longer he lived, the sicker he got, and the more damage he did to himself and his loved ones. That day, all of this was also true about me.

7

"Consumed by pain and rage, at least now I know I am not empty."
-Ashwini Ravi

Over nine years, I became an expert victim. Just as Ralph did not wake up one morning and decide he was going to molest me, I did not make the choice over breakfast one day to suffer abuse. Nevertheless, as years went by, the abuse became routine. There were periods of time I remember better than others and many that used to be vivid and are barely in my memory after healing. I became like a spawning salmon, a puppet, wilting. I had an off switch that Ralph could access. He would touch me; I would turn off. I would submit to his wants. He would touch me while I sat under a blanket watching a movie. I kept sitting under blankets because that is what you do when you watch movies. He asked me to touch his penis on the swingset. I kept pumping my legs because that is what you do on a swingset. When I went into my room alone, he would follow me. I went there anyway, because it was my room. I knew he would lick my nipples and ask me if I liked it, and I wouldn't speak. I froze because nobody taught me what to do when that happened.

I did these things because I believed it would keep the family together. I felt confused, alone, and embarrassed that I was allowing someone to touch me in places I still didn't know the real names of. When we aren't in a safe place, we leave. It's instinct. What do you do when the unsafe place is your own body? What do you do when you are a child who doesn't have the skills to protect yourself? Other girls I knew didn't wear training bras. Other girls I knew didn't keep secrets about their family members. I rationalized that other girls perhaps were not loved like I was. I believed I was the only person that needed to hurt. If I could just endure this pain until I left home, I believed others would be saved from it. I would eventually have a family of my own that was loving, honest, and wanted to spend time together. One day, this would be just a memory, and I would never have to think of it again.

Ralph would give me extra gifts on holidays, and I tried to believe it was a form of love. I received gifts and labeled them as evidence that I was special. Abuse is so manipulative. If I had kept all these mail-order, shined-plastic, glitter-infested symbols of dysfunction, the piles would fill my house. Even as an adult, I received more Christmas money than other family members. I lost the benefits of keeping secrets after I told my family.

Just before I turned eleven, my brother and I took a vacation to Canada with our grandparents. We visited our extended family. We went to a wedding, rode a wooden roller coaster at The World's Fair, and took a ferry to Nanaimo to visit Ralph's sister and brother-in-law. It was the first time I remember being outside Alaska.

My anger finally surfaced during this trip. I was quietly steaming. I snapped at my brother and grandmother and easily hid behind the label of irritable pre-teen. I felt more like a block of ice about to skid into a wall and shatter into still, cold air. I stopped talking to Ralph. I glared at him privately. I sat as far from him as I could without someone asking me why. I did all I could except yell for help. I metaphorically showed my teeth and stayed out of the wolf's den.

We rode horses at my aunt's house where we stayed. We ate fish and rice that my Japanese uncle cooked. They had a pool. Ralph touched me in the pump house when I was changing into my suit, and again under the water. I did not understand how nobody could see that, and it fueled my rage. Outside the pool, I said I was going upstairs and his eyes cracked open the way a crocodile's do when something catches his eye. I will never forget being looked at like that—like I was a tasty morsel for a cold-blooded reptile. I wanted to throw up. My body had been annexed as part of Ralph's territory; I was a prisoner of war dissociated yet unable to leave my body, which would weaponize me against my family if I told them. I wanted to release the pain in a foreign country. I felt lost, numb, and enraged.

I went back inside, put on my pajamas, and climbed into bed. A few minutes later, as usual, Ralph entered and shut the door behind him. I was heartbroken. It didn't matter if I felt nothing and it didn't matter when I got angry. I had taken a huge risk for nothing.

Ralph stopped. He did not come closer than the door. His hands were shaking and he looked like I'd never seen him look before: scared. He resembled a person with emotions, with sadness and grief, like a person with a soul where an addiction had lived; or perhaps they shared the same space and fought over whose side was whose.

He looked at me and said, "I'm sorry. I'm really sorry I hurt you and it will never happen again." He stayed to see if I had anything to say back.

I breathed an, "Okay." He looked like he was going to cry when he turned and left. I felt pressure build in my stomach and my chest as I held my breath and squeezed tightly in a ball, tighter and tighter until I shattered. I sobbed and prayed desperately that he was telling me the truth. I want to say there was a beautiful moment of release and relief, but I stayed in this bone-tired ball and fell asleep. I woke at dinnertime, and I don't remember anything else from that trip. Ralph never touched me again.

The end of this abuse did not mean the end of my suffering. Two months later, at the local high school basketball game, I went to the bathroom and discovered blood in my underwear. I stared at it, mortified. At that moment, the power went out. There was a glow of small, green-tinted emergency lights in the bathroom stall. I thought of *Carrie* and wondered if somehow starting my menstrual cycle had caused a loss of power to the entire building.

I thought, "Why does the world keep taking my body away from me?" I felt despondent that I had gotten my body back for myself just a couple months earlier, and now it was being invaded by a different circumstance. Maybe my body was shedding in blood any memories left inside it. Maybe my body was poisoned and had produced its own poison. Defeated, I sat in the bathroom stall where I held the power of an entire high school's electricity. When a person spends a decade escaping her own body, it is easy to believe it is on a different team or, at best, not working to support her. I stuffed a wad of toilet paper in my underwear and pleaded with God that nobody would see a stain on my plaid pajama pants.

I hid my period for two days, but I had to figure out what

to do before school on Monday. I had collected a pile of blood-stained clothes that I didn't know how to wash under my bed. I told my mom. She was excited. She said something about becoming a woman and celebration and going to lunch while I looked blankly at her. I couldn't comprehend her response. I just wanted to get the pads that would stop me from bleeding all over myself and never talk about it again.

Inside, I was screaming, "I don't want to be a woman! I never got to be a child! This is not beautiful! I don't fucking understand my body and it doesn't feel like something to celebrate!" It would be a long time before I was able to feel safe in my own skin, and during that time, disease developed from the emotions of abuse.

In my mid-twenties, I had a yoga ritual where I would close my eyes and visualize versions of myself from ages 2 to 24 lined up in a field. My present self would stand in front of each one to see who needed my attention the most that day, then invite them to the yoga mat with me. Twelve-year-old Sierra took the longest to agree. For years, she wouldn't make eye contact with me, and she would show up wearing all black while the rest of us were in white. She raged. She found her first survival skill in anger and committed to it.

At 12 years old, I was barely thawing out from being numb. I wasn't being abused anymore, but all the emotions of hopelessness, fear, and anguish became overwhelming when I didn't have the distraction of survival to numb them. I would dress in black and walk into my classroom complaining that it would be another awful day. My favorite song that year was about suicide. When I could get on the internet, I read blogs from people who were depressed, and I read *The Idiot's Guide to Psychology* over and over, diagnosing myself each time. I started cutting my body and experimenting with mixing substances I could find in the medicine cabinet with alcohol. I ate a silica gel packet out of a shoebox, believing it would absorb all the oxygen in my body. I felt clever and was disappointed when I didn't die. I stole cigarettes and put them out on my skin. I stayed in my room alone, writing in journals often.

It was easy to blame my signs on typical pre-teen development. They looked similar, and it is less scary to believe your child, your student, or a young person around you is developing instead of living in extreme pain. Adults weren't talking about the differences between development and mental health symptoms.

That year, we had a standardized writing test. Students would write a short story and it would be sent in for scoring by a panel of teacher judges based on a rubric. I wrote a story called Euphoric Field and I received a perfect score. It was a narrative told from the perspective of a sister whose brother had completed suicide. I told a lot of my own story in the little boy's tale, but hid inside the differences between us. I remember sitting in the computer lab typing. I was there longer than any of my classmates—the last one done. I spoke of the field I imagined in my head—that I still imagine in my head—as an escape. My story was red-flagged for adult content. I remember being congratulated many times for receiving a perfect score. I don't remember being asked why I chose to write about suicide.

During this year, a friend that I had confided in about the abuse reported it to the school nurse. At the time, I felt a mix of betrayal that she had told, fear the nurse would talk to me, and repressed hope that someone would help me and it wouldn't be my choice. I was called to the nurse's office and she told me what had been reported and that she would need to tell my parents. She asked me directly if it was true and I denied it, simultaneously hoping both that she would believe me and that she wouldn't.

I couldn't allow myself to be the one to tell. I couldn't allow it to be my choice. I was petrified that telling the truth would betray my family, not only because it would condemn my grandfather, but because the rest of my family would be hurt.

My dad tells me stories about taking me for drives so I might feel more comfortable talking about it. I believe this happened, but I have no memory of it. Later, I would learn he confronted Ralph about it and asked him directly if it happened. Ralph denied it. He lied to his son to save himself from the consequences.

My parents knew I was cutting myself. They knew something was off. They asked me to go to therapy and I refused. I said I was fine. They went to therapists to ask what to do. They were told it would be reported to the state and they may investigate it. In hindsight, this may seem like an obvious choice, but when you are in it, that isn't how it feels. Do you choose to go down a road that assumes your daughter is lying and drags your own father through the mud when both of them have denied anything happened?

They took me to the doctor and I reported feeling depressed. I took some St John's Wart supplement for a time, but I was too far in the situation for it to help. They were doing everything they knew to do and didn't have the information they needed, either from me or Ralph, or information on the signs and symptoms of abuse. My dad often says parents need to get educated and talk about what to look for. It's easy to think abuse could never happen to our own children. We hear stories about other people and believe we are protected; it's hard to consider we might not be—that our kids might not be. It opens us up for shame that we have failed as parents and family members.

Every time they tried to get me to talk, I wanted them to know, but I felt so unsafe I lashed out. I was angry and I felt like it was too late. It had ended. I needed their help before that and I was furious it was coming after the fact. To me at 12 years old, they had waited too long. I didn't understand the aftermath or that I still needed help. If nobody had helped me before, I told myself, they would not be helping me now. I believed speaking out would make my life worse; kids would talk about me, my family would talk about me, I would have to talk to a therapist or a police officer, and all of these people would see me as broken. During that time, I believed I was. I believed the only way to end the pain was to end my life.

The hunting rifle was mounted next to the door during moose season. Since we lived in the middle of the woods, a bull moose might come into the yard and we would have some meat for the winter. I planned to use this gun in an attempt one day and waited for my family to leave. As soon as they were out of the driveway, I went to the porch where the gun hung, but it wasn't there. I was disappointed and fixated on finding it. I scoured the house, searching in boxes, cabinets, closets, in the basement, and in storage. I knew it had to be somewhere in the house. Without it, I would have to keep living in constant suffering. I ended up self-harming and falling asleep. I was devastated. My parents saved my life by locking up their gun that day.

I attempted suicide thirteen times that year. I was obsessed with it. I was writing about it, thinking about it, researching it in secret, waiting for any time that I could be alone to try again, and each time feeling disappointed that my methods didn't work. My parents were worried, monitoring my internet use, noticing my behavior, considering if I was hanging out with friends that weren't healthy, and probably more than I knew. I became an expert at hiding and justifying my behavior, making it easier to attribute to typical development. I knew how to perform at school for grades, I played sports, started band, and in many ways did not look like an adult’s idea of an abused child. I marketed the role of a typical angsty teen to buy time until I died. My parents were so close to the truth.

I was provided a lot of protective factors. I engaged in activities outside of school and was involved in a healthy community. I lived in a small place where people knew me and talked to me in public. I had a teacher who I believe was more helpful to me than anything else. Patricia taught me math, reading, and writing. I had gotten to know her in these pull-out classes for a few years by then. She would teach us French and bake homemade eclairs as special treats. She would bring cinnamon candy canes with hot cocoa in December and she would validate my feelings when I was upset. As a child, I couldn't articulate why I loved her, but it was because she treated her students like humans. She loved us more than the schoolwork we did with her and it was clear in her interactions.

Patricia spoke to us when we lacked gratitude for the treats she brought us, she told us stories about her times living in France, about smoking cigarettes, and about other topics many adults would avoid. She normalized people of any age making mistakes, having feelings, and not having it all figured out. I felt seen as an individual and I felt loved by her. On some level, I concluded that if Patricia loved me, I was somehow worthy of love, even when I didn't feel it.

When I left that school, Patricia would make appearances in my life from time to time. We would have tea, I would help her organize her kitchen cabinets, and I would invite her to graduations. As a child, I didn't confide to her that I was abused or that I was in so much pain. When she wasn't around, I would often think about her and use her love as hope that one day I could see in myself what she saw in me. It was the first time I considered that life could be different; even though I wasn't aware at the time, it was a gift she gave me that stayed somewhere in me. I believe in many ways that I can never know how Patricia saved my life and kept me from making more painful decisions later on.

In my twenties, I was able to visit Patricia and tell her how much she helped me during that time. She didn't know I had experienced abuse or the aftermath. It didn't matter, because she was able to love me the same way without that information. We never know how we impact others unless they tell us. As an adult, I have been able to reach out to many teachers from my childhood because I felt like I had permission to do so from knowing Patricia. Keeping adults of all ages in my life, asking them questions, sharing my experiences, and hearing about theirs has been immeasurably valuable to me.

People of all ages are teachers. We can't know who might show up to support us or who we may be supporting at any stage in life.

8

"Travel isn't always pretty. It isn't always comfortable. Sometimes it hurts, it even breaks your heart. But that's okay. The journey changes you; it should change you. It leaves marks on your memory, on your consciousness, on your heart, and on your body. You take something with you. Hopefully, you leave something good behind."
–Anthony Bourdain

By the time I reached high school, I had mastered the game of public school. I performed so well that I was participating in all the advanced classes, playing varsity sports, serving as president of my class, and singing in honor choir. I knew what people wanted, expected, graded, and I did it well. It was not because I always worked hard—though I did for some things—but because I learned the rules well enough to know when I could break them. I knew how to take multiple choice tests based on the answers offered, I knew how to write a book report without reading the book, and I knew how to get people to like themselves around me so they thought they liked me. I was a master manipulator like many addicts or people who have been abused before. We learn from the best.

Manipulation is not a negative skill like we often believe. It is a neutral tool that we often use to reach a desirable outcome. After accomplishing everything I thought public school had to offer me, I was bored. I felt like I had three more years of nowhere to go, so I made the smartest decision I ever made as a teenager and announced to my parents I was going to participate in the foreign exchange program. They responded that this was an unsafe idea that wasn't going to happen. I had not considered the possibility of them not agreeing and, at first, felt confused that this was happening.

I experienced what I call Straight-A Student Syndrome, or SASS, that I learned from growing up in the public school system. When you fulfill (or appear to fulfill) all the expectations of a model student in school, you often gain the trust to do things that others don't get to do. Teachers stop telling you no. I also didn't feel like my parents truly knew who I was, so I didn't often consider their opinions in making decisions. I felt stunned by this new obstacle I hadn't considered.

I imagined going to parties and drinking, maybe using drugs and seeing what else was there for me in high school. I was convinced that if I stayed in Alaska I would use drugs and get into trouble. I thought my dream of traveling was over. I immediately started planning my manipulation. I got a job that I could work over the summer and part-time during school. I signed up for online classes that I would need to complete if I missed them while abroad. I researched all the program options, chose the best one, decided where to go, calculated I would need to work 18 months to save the money to go, and applied. I received an email of acceptance from the program that required my parents' signatures to move forward.

There was a mix of pride and defeat on my parents' faces as I showed them this letter of acceptance and explained to them my step-by-step plan to pay for and travel to Brazil for an entire year of high school. I'm sure they discussed this in private before deciding, but all I remember is staring wide-eyed as my dad shrugged his shoulders and said, "I guess you're going to Brazil."

Over the next year-and-a-half, I worked hard, saved money, played sports, kept singing in choir, went to class in person and online, and as I predicted, drank and smoked pot. The goal of travel alongside the busyness of my schedule kept me focused enough to avoid intentionally making big mistakes. Luck kept me from unintentionally making them.

During this time, I had a relationship with a man I loved dearly. He was eight years older than me and broke up with me because he was at a different place in his life, as you can imagine. I was devastated and had no emotional regulation to soothe the pain. It triggered abandonment and insecurity that I had experienced as a child and added to the unprocessed emotions already suffocating me. I started drinking more often and smoking pot every night. I just needed to make it another six months to escape the country.

On Halloween, I was cut early from my shift at work. Any unplanned free time was painful to me. It left me without a distraction, and distractions were my survival plan for high school. I played some drinking games with my coworkers and later decided to drive to my ex-boyfriend's house. I knocked on his door and he answered, probably expecting a trick-or-treating child, but found me standing there, cute and bubbly; desperate and buzzed. We exchanged some shallow conversation as I tried to ease my way into spending time with him and he tried to ease his way out of it.

"I'm busy right now," he said as I looked down to see a pair of women's shoes on the floormat. The realization that he was with another woman crushed me, brought me straight back into sobriety, and silenced the small talk.

"Oh sure, okay, have fun," I turned and walked away, thinking I didn't want him to have fun at all. I had to get out of this situation. I got into my car and drove down the driveway, focused on getting drunk. Stored in my car was a bottle of vodka that I opened and started to sip. If I started drinking now, I decided, there would be a certain amount of time for which I would be fine to drive before it hit me. However, I was in flight mode and kept driving, deciding at each turn to take another sip, and impulsively choosing which way to go. I came to a stop sign and turned right. Seconds later, I saw the red-and-blue lights flashing to pull me over. With one hand on the steering wheel and the other holding the vodka and shifting, I didn't have time to twist the lid on or pop a breath mint in my mouth. I propped the bottle up in my passenger seat and threw a sweatshirt over it.

I knew I was done for. I must have swerved. He must have been following me for some time. I probably smelled like alcohol and I had an open bottle sitting right next to me while I was driving. I saw myself getting arrested, my parents getting angry, and worst of all, my escape to South America slipping from my grasp.

I was staring into space thinking how nothing mattered anymore when the officer approached my window. I gave him my license and registration and he asked if I knew why he pulled me over as he shone his flashlight over the hidden alcohol and my sweatshirt. I said no. He told me I didn't come to a complete stop at the sign.

"What? I thought I did. I'm sorry. I didn't see anyone coming," I was shocked. He went to run my information and I waited for him to come back and tell me I smelled like alcohol to get out of the truck.

"Here you go. I know there aren't many people here and you can see traffic at the sign, but just make sure you come to a complete stop next time. Count to one or two at the stop sign. I'm not going to give you a ticket this time. Be safe," he turned and walked away. I let my breath go and rolled up my window, put my truck in first gear and spoke out loud, "Go straight. Drive straight. You can do it." I turned off the road as soon as I could and returned to my friends' house.

Later that night, the same officer and his colleague came to investigate a noise complaint at the apartment.

"I saw you earlier tonight," he said to me.

"You did. That was before I came here, and I haven't gone anywhere since then." I felt like I was pleading with him. We told him we had a couple of drinks but had not gone anywhere, and I was asleep when he arrived, so he let me go for the second time. I'd had just enough time to black out from drinking and sleep most of it off between the two times I saw him.

I played the game of school well, and that night, I played the game of the law well enough. I didn't tell my parents that I needed to go to Brazil because I was going to become an addict if I stayed, but that night, I was certain it would have been true.

I made it to January and flew to Porto Alegre, Brazil via Anchorage, Los Angeles, Brasilia, and Rio de Janeiro. In the Anchorage airport, my parents and all my friends who had come to say goodbye were lined up across the window, and I could see them from the tiny Dash-8 plane I had boarded. I started to sob. All the love I had was waving goodbye to me and I doubted whether I should be running away from it, but I couldn't stand the thought of staying, either.

It took two days to get to Brazil. I went from ice and snow to 95-degree sun and humidity. I walked out of the airport and gasped, feeling like I couldn't breathe. My host dad drove us home while my host sister translated for me. We drove down a red cobblestone street faster than what felt safe while swerving around a mule pulling a cart of recyclables, and that scene felt like a quintessential visual for the change I had agreed upon for this year.

Everything there was opposite of what I knew before: heat, humidity, white sand, a huge city, gated homes, a Catholic school, tiny clothes, public transportation, air conditioning instead of heaters, summer in January, winter in July… and suddenly I didn't know the rules for anything. My host family was amazing. We spent time on the coast first, then went back to the city for school. My oldest host sister spoke English and translated for me during the first few months I was there.

Three weeks after I arrived, my sisters and I went to a nightclub called Ibiza to celebrate Carnival. This Alaskan girl didn't know what a nightclub was, especially since we just called it "Ibiza." What I knew was that we would take a bus with our friends, stay all night, then take the bus home in the morning. It was safer to spend the night somewhere than travel through the night there. My instructions were clear enough: wear dancing shoes, stay with your sisters, and the more glitter you can put on your face, the better.

I was unprepared for all parts of this night: the large party bus, the club with several rooms themed with décor and music, and especially the culture. I was dancing my booty off in a hip hop-themed room when a boy—who may have been a man, but I'll call him a boy—started to dance with me. By dance with, I mean grind on my leg or backside while I kept moving a step away from him and he kept closing the gap. I told him I wanted to dance by myself. He ignored me.

I went to my sister and told her, “Hey, I can't communicate with this guy. Can you tell him that I don't speak Portuguese?” My sis said something and the boy replied, then continued to vibrate his hips against my side like a backwards bobblehead doll. I wasn't moving at all anymore as I looked at my sister with eyebrows raised, questioning what was going on.

“He said it's okay that you don't speak Portuguese because he doesn't want to talk to you,” she said apologetically. “Let's go to another room.” I nodded, peeling my leg back from Bobblehips, then walking backwards with my arms out to keep him away like a dog that wouldn't stop jumping on me. He followed me until I crossed the doorway.

This was the first time I learned that “no” meant “try harder,” and it reinforced the idea that my body was there to serve men. Long after I became fluent, I would use the excuse of not speaking Portuguese many times to avoid men I didn't feel safe with, and I told them I was from Argentina and only spoke Spanish. It made me close enough not to be a vulnerable target, but far enough away for them to lose interest.

We traveled to the countryside to visit some family who owned a farm in Cascavel—which means Rattlesnake—and you could hear them rattle in the forest at night with the lightning bugs glowing across the fields. After dinner, one of the goats came in and got up on the table to eat the leftovers. I think my host family thought this was stranger than I did. I was enamored with the South American farm life, yet unprepared for snakes or other dangers I had never heard of. We fished in the pond and rode horses before we continued our trip.

Our next stop was Paraguay, where we only stayed for a few hours to buy things from the street shops. Specifically, we went for luggage that my sister and I would travel with. Fifteen years later, I still use the one I bought that day.

When we arrived, a boy who looked about ten years old appeared next to us, waving. My host dad nodded back at him and the boy began running in front of our car. My confusion turned to concern when I realized the boy was barefoot on the dirt road. I cringed at the thought of blisters on his toes and the heat burning the bottom of his feet as he led us up a short hill to a parking place. My host dad tipped him with some cash and on he went, waving, then running back down the hill to direct the next car. I wondered if this was common for children, if this was what poverty looked like, or if running all day helped his health and wealth.

In Argentina, we visited Iguazu Falls. We sang national anthems for every country we knew in the car and marveled at how each of them made us feel; not understanding all the words in English, Portuguese, French, and some Italian, we were left with tone and candor.

The Falls were beautiful and impressive in size. There are between 150 and 300 falls there. I bought some postcards before we walked down the 180 stairs to admire the water. All over the park, there were small mammals called quatis that looked like a cross between a raccoon and an anteater. They had been conditioned to beg for food like many park-living animals, and the sound of my bag of postcards drew them near to be pet and adored. They left, disappointed by my lack of potato chips.

The water crashed powerfully as we stood next to it. From several yards away, we could feel the mist and imagine the weight of the falls hitting the pool beneath. We had to yell to each other to be able to hear over it. There were countless rainbows of various sizes in every direction, butterflies fluttering through the air, alligators basking beneath us, and hundreds of people of varying ethnicities capturing the beauty of nature with their cameras.

Living in Brazil was difficult. I experienced quite a bit of culture shock. Some people didn't like me because I was American and they would ask me why I loved George W. Bush, then quietly walk away when I told them I didn't. It was noticeably different to introduce myself as Alaskan rather than American. I fell asleep at school quite a bit because it was exhausting to try to understand Portuguese well enough to do schoolwork. My parents would send me packages of peanut butter, canned salmon, and chocolate chips to make cookies with. Brazil didn't have these things in the store. My classmates were excited for me to make cookies because their cookies were different, kind of dry and hard like Oreos.

My life was full of the distractions I had sought out so I didn't feel pain. I was far away from my family and spent my time at the gym, reading comic books, and watching television with subtitles on so I could learn the language. After two months, I could speak well enough to start taking the bus and learning how to get to other places. After six months, I took an Italian language class with my host mom. After ten months, I started to forget words in English.

My family there was generous and supportive. We had a small pool, two dogs, and when my host mom went back to school to study law, we had a housekeeper. I remember she asked me where my laundry was because I kept doing it myself, not knowing how to allow someone to clean for me. My host grandmother would stay with us often on weekends. She lived in an apartment and had parrots. She would make black beans for the week in a pressure cooker every Sunday. Each meal in Brazil is served with beans and rice. I ate that almost every day for over a year and never got tired of it. I loved my host family, but I struggled to accept everything they offered me; looking back at it, I believe it was hard to fully trust them and allow myself to be vulnerable. There was so much change in my life, and I had come from a family in which I felt disconnected from experiences that I didn't know how to live without.

It was hard to connect with friends in Brazil. A lot of kids my age liked to shop, hang out at malls, and play sports I had never played, and I didn't know how to engage in a city, let alone overcome the cultural difference. I had one wonderful friend named Camila who went to school with me and lived just a few streets away. She took the time to explain things to me when I couldn't speak well in class.

The first time I called her on the phone, she was surprised. "Who is this? Sierra?! You are calling me on the phone!" I had written out a script to ask for her and invite her to hang out with me so we would have the details correct. Camila was dedicated to helping me understand and feel included while I lived there. She would walk with me and explain how society worked and where different places were. She invited me to cultural activities such as Gaúcho dancing or her parents' traditional Churrascaria restaurant. Camila was the only other teenager in my class who had never been robbed in public. She told me how to avoid this by wearing my backpack on the front and never answering strangers who asked what time it is. I still have notes she wrote me in class. We both have grown to teach yoga and travel the world.

At the end of October, I was able to purchase a ticket to Manaus, the capital city in the Northwest, closest to the Amazon rainforest. I took a boat trip on the Rio Negro for seven days and spent the other three in the city. As we were landing in Manaus, I realized I had left my wallet with all my money at home. As if I brought the quaintness of Alaska with me, there happened to be a man on the flight who was a family friend, and he let me borrow enough money for my trip and pay him back when I returned. I felt so lucky that he decided to go fishing that same day and had the resources to lend me.

While Porto Alegre was the tenth-largest city in Brazil with over 4 million people, Manaus was even larger. Like in many countries, Brazilians look different according to their region and history of settlers. I had adapted to city life and had had enough time to tan my skin that I looked like I was from another part of the country rather than a complete foreigner. People told me I sounded like I was from the West Coast. The food was similar but had different seasonings, and the people mostly had darker skin and slimmer body types. I ate empanadas from street carts, walked through long stretches of colorful marketplaces on the river, and admired street artists creating incredible paintings on tiles with their fingers.

I spent one night in a hotel and left my suitcase there to catch my boat the next morning. The first time I saw the river, it was huge, murky, and had lots of cruise boat traffic at the mouth—very different from Alaskan waters. To the southwest flowed the Rio Branco and to the north the Rio Negro, intersecting near the port of Manaus. I met my group and we boarded a smaller boat—about 50 square feet with two decks. It had a dining area and a room for the Native family who cooked and drove the boat to sleep in. We slept in hammocks on the top deck. One night when it was very windy, we stayed in a cabin on the shore.

Our group was made up of seven people whom I adored. There was a couple from Denmark who were traveling the world together; the woman would not get married until she was thirty and her boyfriend was waiting for that day. There was an older couple from Britain who skipped some activities to rest. There was a couple from California who worked in the film industry, and I still keep in touch with them. They were fascinated by me because I was the youngest and the only solo traveler, and because I knew things like diner breakfast lingo, how to fillet a salmon, and Portuguese. It was a special group of people to spend a week with.

We explored in the most incredible, authentic way I could have hoped for. My favorite night was when we slept in the jungle in our hammocks with mosquito nets. We roasted whole chickens on the fire with rice and beans. As night fell and we lied down, I heard snakes, bugs, birds, and then a raspy growl as we were going to sleep. I whispered to our guide in Portuguese to ask what it was without alarming anyone else.

He said, "It's a leopard. It probably smells the chicken we

made."

"Oh! That is really cool. I wish I could have seen it," I responded, then fell instantly asleep the way only a young adult without fear of the wild would.

We hiked to waterfalls and found an impressively rich variety of animals including parrots, tucans, giant trap door spiders, and orb spiders. We pulled on a piece of web as hard as we could and could not break it. It was said to be stronger than a ten-cord rope. We found boa constrictors, sloths, pink dolphins, and blue morpho butterflies. I will never forget standing in the rainforest when that butterfly flew past us. Time stopped for that millisecond and nothing made a sound until it fluttered away. It was the most beautiful thing I have seen in nature. We went crocodile sighting at night with headlamps and saw their eyes slinking across the water. We watched venus in the night sky and fished for piranhas with bamboo poles and raw pork, then ate them for dinner. They were the boniest fish I had ever eaten.

We visited a village of Native people who spoke Portuguese, the language of their tribe, and a universal tribe language to communicate with others who traveled near them. Tribes there used to be nomadic. They would mark trees and had sound patterns to detect who was around and to signal for danger. They fed their young milky sap that came from the trees and weaved bags out of giant fronds to carry things in. They foraged for food and hunted animals with vine traps. They showed us all these ways of life and yet, like many Native tribes, the modern world had pushed them out of this lifestyle. They now lived in one place and were visited enough to have a hut with souvenirs like feather earrings and crocodile-tooth necklaces. There was a makeshift school for children and they wore modern clothing which they would trade for or buy from the city. To make money, they sold mandioca root, which is tapioca or cassava, and when it was hard, they would cut down trees and sell the wood on the black market. Nobody had taught them how to farm, so their mandioca crops were small and unsuited for the land it grew on.

We got our faces painted in traditional patterns for celebrations and hunting trips with pollen and berry stains. We hiked to a waterfall where some of the tribe members washed laundry and bathed. We washed our hair in the river. We had to scan each others' bodies every time we went into the water to make sure we didn't have any water ticks in our skin. I had a water tick that we pulled out with tweezers.

We watched the sunrise and the sunset on the river; it was vast with shades of pink, yellow, orange, red, and blue. I loved it in the rainforest and on the river. It was like a magical place that was almost untouched by humans. I felt like I was in a fairytale where creatures could talk and life was palpably symbiotic. I was grateful that mother nature allowed me the opportunity to be there, and I felt sad for the sandwich stacks of ferry boats that would only go as far as the narrowing river would allow. They saw only what was made specifically for tourists, like tamed dolphin resorts or a lodges off the shore without ants, and they could not lean over the railing to touch the water from their decks.

Our river guide was more than friendly to me. In fact, he claimed he fell in love with me. He asked me many times to stay in his boat room, but I declined. He would flirt with me in Portuguese so his other clients wouldn't find him unprofessional. The family that cooked for us stayed on the boat and giggled at him when I turned him down in Portuguese during dinner. He tried to touch me when we stayed in the cabin and twice in the hammock after dark. I wouldn't let him. I told him he couldn't be in love with me; he had just met me, and I wasn't interested. At the time, I was so desensitized to the idea that "no means try harder" that it felt normal to spend so much time repeating no to him. Now it is clear to me that this is harassment, but back then, it was what I had always known.

The last day, we went to the Meeting of the Waters of the Rio Negro and the Rio Branco. The pH levels, silt mix, salinity, and temperature created a distinct color that was always there. I could feel the change from one side to the other through the water on my fingers. When we got off the boat, our group made a plan to meet for dinner that night.

Strangely, we met at an Italian restaurant in the heart of the Amazonas. Our guide, Conrado, invited me to walk around town and go dancing afterward. I knew his intentions were not the same as mine. I also knew I was not going to walk around the city alone after dark. Still, I desperately wanted to see the night life of the city and go dancing. I had planned to meet my California friends to tour the Opera House the next morning, so they would report it if anything went wrong, but that thought never crossed my mind. I thought I would spend the evening avoiding his flirting and ignoring advances while seeing a place I may never get to see again.

We walked to town square and saw street performers painted in different colors, guitar players singing, men performing capoeira, and jugglers. Sweet smells of fried bananas and manioca pancakes with nuts and butter filled the air.

I was drinking beer on our walk to the club, excited to see traditional dances of this region. People were flipping and twirling dizzily when we arrived. I had learned some Samba from my parents, which was much easier for me than the fast-paced Forró happening that night. I kept drinking and spinning, following my lead to step one way and then the other, shimmy my hips to the side, to the front, back, side, back, front, back, twirl, twirl back, twirl around, to the back, front, and on and on. I was enamored and exhilarated to be shown and led in a dance like this. It was challenging and required my focus to step correctly, but the beer eradicated my fear that people were staring at me, even though they were definitely staring. This club was a serious dance club and I was not only a beginner, but also a first-timer. I was having a blast and we were out until 4 a.m. dancing together, which is a normal-to-early curfew in Brazil.

We returned to my hotel room, and by then, I was drunk and exhausted. The front desk person looked at Conrado, who went over to say something while I waited for the elevator, then came up to my room with me. I laid down on the bed, he turned the TV on, and I fell asleep.

I woke up to Conrado having sex with me. I opened my eyes, saw his face, started peeing on him, then projectile-vomited across the bed. My body immediately rejected the situation, as well as much of the beer I drank while spinning in circles for hours that night. He jumped off the bed and asked if I was okay.

"Get out." I glared at him, watched him put his pants on, and waited for the door to shut behind him before I rolled to a dry part of the bed and passed out again.

I woke up two hours later to the beep of my alarm, hurried through a blurry shower, and ran downstairs to meet my friends in a cab in front of the hotel. They asked how my night was. I told them I had a blast dancing and was still a bit drunk. I said nothing about waking up to being raped.

The tour of the Opera House was beautiful and the concert blew my mind. I went on with my day as if nothing out of the ordinary happened. It felt as though I was going through the motions of a typical experience. In many ways, it felt exactly the same as it had years ago—my body was used without my permission, and I shoved the emotions deep down, then took a shower and went on with my day.

For years, I thought it was my fault. I had made the choices that led up to that; agreeing to spend time with him alone, getting drunk, and not stopping him from coming up to my hotel room. I even felt wrong for falling asleep, as if it were my job to keep my guard up; as if my body were public land unless I was conscious to defend it. I never told my host family or my biological family. The first person I told was my boyfriend three years later. He replied, "Why did you let him up to your hotel room? Why are you telling me this?" We got in a fight about it because he thought it was insensitive of me to tell him about a previous sexual experience I had.

For years, I included Conrado in the number of people I had had sex with. Now, I count him in the number of people who have raped me. Nothing I did was an invitation for him to screw me while I slept, no matter how much he claimed to be in love with me or misunderstand the countless times I told him not to touch me during the week we were together.

I was in Manaus for another day and a half. He left me a note at the front desk of my hotel when I was out shopping that night, then showed up the next morning when I was leaving for breakfast. He invited me to go with him. I said no and he asked if I was okay. He didn't understand that he had raped me. He lived in a culture that taught him "no means try harder" and believed I could somehow give consent in my drunken and sleeping state. I told him I was fine and walked into a large crowd, turned several corners, and watched to make sure he wasn't following. I never saw Conrado again.

I used to feel devastated for countries that condone rape as commonplace, arrange marriages for teenage girls with men twice their ages, and sell women and children to the porn industry. I felt sad for every place where saying no was a challenge and consent was something most people couldn't define. Now I realize the United States is one of those countries. I tried to contact the agency Conrado worked for years later to tell him—just in case he was still there, possibly raping other tourists—but they were either out of business or I didn't remember the name correctly.

Before I flew back to Porto Alegre, I bought some paintings from a man who sold them on the sidewalk. I remember sitting on the plane thinking the best week of my life had been stained with the awful choices I had made. I was angry and full of self-loathing, mortified that my memory of this perfect trip had been infiltrated by the memory of having sex with someone I didn't want to have sex with. Sex was something so personal, confusing, and intimate to me that I couldn't understand or admit to myself how badly I felt.

I am grateful that some people do not understand what

it's like to shower over and over again, scrubbing their bodies raw to wash off the pain they are left with, to try to escape their own skin like a layer of scum from the rapes that their hearts cannot shed. On the flight home, I dissociated with my body and the memory, as if I could put it in the vault of secrets I never needed to share again. It didn't matter that everything around me was completely different from Alaska; everything inside me was the same.

9

"The conflict between the will to deny horrible events and the will to proclaim them aloud is the central dialectic of psychological trauma."
-Judith Lewis Herman

The year my grandmother died, I had distanced myself from my family to focus on healing. By the time I visited her, she was hovering between life and death. I didn't know what to say or if it was wrong to tell her about my disappointment while she was on her deathbed. I was torn between validating my desire not to be around my family and wishing they would talk to me about my experiences, which was an obstacle to beginning the grieving process for the loss of my grandmother.

She called me over while I was visiting for the last time. "Sierra, I hope you find love, get married, and are happy in life," she said. I listened as she discussed things that seemed insignificant to me. "I really like Luke. He is a good guy," she said, referring to my ex-boyfriend, picking through layers of an open wound; I wasn't dating him anymore, and all she had to offer me was her wish that a man would come along to make me happy? I wanted to ask what kind of happily-ever-after her husband had given her. I kept my sarcastic comments to myself.

"Thanks, Grandma," I replied, curious as to what would come next.

"Who are all these people standing in this room?" She pointed around her living room.

"I don't know who they are, Grandma. I believe you can see them, but I can't. They must be here to visit with you."

"Oh," she paused, "oh." Then she was back in transition. I don't remember the last thing I said to my grandmother. When she died, the sadness and heartache were echoes I could hardly feel.

My family speaks about her like she was the savior of us all. I think that was probably true for some, but all I felt was betrayal, at the time. I was angry that my family hadn't been there for me, and she was part of that. I was angry that she was too nice to consider how she was enabling harm. I didn't know about her childhood, her history, or anything that would justify this to me. She loved dancing, baking, hockey, and collecting hockey cards. The most personal thing I knew about her was that she secretly smoked cigarettes in the cellar downstairs. I had found her pack there once and giggled at the idea of her hiding a habit from the rest of a family that had the same one. There was comfort for me in knowing something she felt she had to hide, and I wondered what else she hid about herself.

Her humanity came through to me in bits and pieces. She knitted and crocheted treasures to give away and sell at craft fairs. She wore a wig even before her hair started thinning, and the young cousins in Canada would put it on when she visited. We laughed at the images of toddlers with thick, medium-length feathered hairstyles from the '70s. I never heard her say a negative thing about anyone beyond the banter of hockey teams that would lose to the Pittsburgh Penguins or how her cribbage opponent was going down. When she was in the hospital, she told my dad to burn Ralph. She said to set him on fire and let him burn. I don't know how much of that was her voice and how much was the effect of the drugs they had given her.

After her memorial in September, I flew home and drove straight to the woods. I knew my favorite memories of her were all in the moss and berries. I picked cranberries in the bog, plunking them into my plastic bucket. I spoke to her out loud, told her of my empty grief and disappointment, then cried that I felt disconnected from her. Finally, I came to what I loved about her most. She loved people. Her kind, gentle spirit came from love, and I wanted to model that in my life. By not having them, she had taught me that boundaries were essential and love came out of stating what we needed and taking responsibility for our own happiness. Marriage did not give her fulfillment, and it would not give me happiness. I made a commitment to master her compassion and add my own loving boundaries in my lifetime. I said goodbye to her as the wind gusted through the bog.

Throughout that month, I spent many nights wrapped in blankets, considered how to be compassionate with boundaries. I reflected on my responsibility as an adult learning to care for my child self. One conclusion I came to was that Ralph was still alive and still had a driver's license, so the possibility of other children being harmed by him remained. I decided I would report the abuse I had experienced to the police as a form of loving protection of other children in the world. I wanted Ralph to have consequences, but I didn't know what those would be, nor did I believe it was my responsibility to dole them out. I would allow the law to do its job.

I had been jumping from place to place, house sitting for people for two years. People kept asking, so I had put my things in storage and enjoyed having temporary pets and homes. I had found a small house for sale by owner that summer, put in an offer, and was set to have my own home in the fall.

I drove to the police station and walked in to stand at the little glass window. “Hi,” I smiled, “I want to make a report. I've never done that before.”

“What are you reporting?” The woman inside the box responded.

“Childhood sexual abuse.”

“How do you know the victim?”

“Oh, I am the...survivor. I'm reporting something from the past that was never reported.”

“Okay. If you sit over there, I will bring you the paperwork to fill out.”

“Okay, thank you,” I smiled a second time, assumably twice more than anyone else who was in a police station to report abuse. I sat in one of two chairs in the entryway until she came out with a clipboard and some forms. The chair uncomfortably hugged my hips on either side and I wondered how anyone bigger than me could sit there. I wrote my information and a general description of what happened, then brought the forms back to the window.

“Anytime a woman is involved in abuse, we do the interviews at the women's shelter. They will call you and schedule a time for you to go there and speak with an advocate,” she explained.

The sergeant of the station, Larry, walked up at that moment. “Hey, I know you; you're Clayton and Michelle's daughter?" I wondered if he had seen me on a camera and come to visit.

"That's right, Sierra," I smiled yet again.

"Yeah, I remember you were really great at softball, and I've seen you for a long time. I haven't read this, but I know you wouldn't be here if you didn't need help, and that's my job. She explained you will go to the women's shelter next. If you have any questions or want to talk, you can call this number to my extension." This was the first of many times I would wait in limbo for the next step. I felt comforted that Larry had come down, embarrassed that he would read this story about me, and fearful that he would think my parents were bad people. I thanked him for his number and left.

A few days later, I walked into the shelter and sat on a couch in what looked like a living room. I had known the advocate who met me there for many years, because that is the nature of a small town. She let me know I was being videotaped and there was a police officer in another room who would watch as I was interviewed. I answered questions and described the details of the abuse. Telling this story felt routine and unemotional at the time. I was reciting facts, but how I felt about them was irrelevant to the purpose of the interview; though, as I spoke, my advocate friend validated what I was saying without trying to lead me anywhere. The justice system seems to balance between avoiding the tactics that bring victims in (such as gaslighting and invalidation) and maintaining neutrality regarding the perpetrator. These skills are different, yet they bleed into each other readily, nuanced by subjective perception.

When I left, I sobbed. I felt all the emotions that were irrelevant to the legal process, especially sadness for the little girl who experienced mistrust, betrayal, confusion, and isolation. I felt a familiar sense of ambivalence, seeing her as a little girl outside myself yet feeling her experience first-hand.

I drove away in this detached fog and picked up some thai food on the way home. This was the first night I was able to stay in my own home. Nothing had been moved in and there were leftovers from a long stint of bachelorhood in my home: 1970s dishware, amber-colored glasses, huge stereo speakers, mint walls, and an even worse pastel pink in the bedroom. Every corner of the house was dusty and few of them had square angles. It would have seemed like this was not my space, and it's true that the house was in transition, but it was mine. I walked in, set my things down, and opened a box of coarse salt and started pouring it along the edges of each room until the entryway, kitchen, hall, bathroom, stairs, and doorways were lined. The entire house was sitting in a salt barrier. I rolled the borrowed sleeping bag out over a sheepskin rug to create a nest for myself.

I walked the perimeter of the house, first outside and then inside, repeating, "This home welcomes healthy and loving relationship. All inside experience joy, support, play, creativity, and safety. I can decide who I allow in and none shall pass without respect and safety in their heart." I said versions of this over and over as I paced through my home.

As I fell asleep in my nest after recalling all my memories in an interview, I felt the warmth of having my own shelter and knew I was safe for the first time in my life.

The next week, I received a call from the police. They explained that because it had been so long since the abuse took place, we needed a confession if I wanted to move forward in the legal process. I would need to go to the station, call Ralph on the phone, and get him to admit to the abuse while our conversation was being recorded. I recognized the sensation from telling my mom as a small child that I was being abused—if I spoke, I would betray my family, I could potentially open a long and difficult legal process, and I had to do this in front of a stranger. This time, I didn't feel responsible for taking care of everyone else. I was responsible for giving the information I had and letting it go.

I had a window of time to go to the station and make this call on a Saturday. This was the most daunting chore I had undertaken. I was chanting internal pep talks the entire drive there. When I arrived, an officer met me and led me up some stairs to his office. I sat across from him at his desk with the phone on speaker. My legs were shaking. The officer was dry and direct.

When he asked, I let him know I had told my parents I was going through this process. He shook his head at me; "We told you not to do that because often the perpetrator will get word and he won't tell the truth," he scolded. In this room, there was no more validation or empathy about how difficult this process was for me.

I dictated the number and my uncle answered. "Hey! Oh, no he isn't here. I think he went to the store. He should be back in a couple hours…" As he kept talking, I tried telepathically to tell him to shut up because he was being recorded at a police station. I didn't know what incriminating thing he might say, but I was certain he would say it in that moment. As soon as he stopped talking, I ended the conversation and said I would call back.

The officer looked at me snidely. "See? I told you. You can come back later and try again, I guess." I was screaming and cursing at him in my head: *Are you fucking kidding me? That is your response to what just happened? 'I told you so?' Have you ever had to do this before? Have you ever called your family member to trick them into admitting they committed a crime so they would have to go to court while an inconsiderate, insensitive jerk of a police officer sat across the desk and looked at you like you were the stupidest little girl who ever lived?!!! Can you even consider how terrifying this is for me right now?! Sergeant Larry likes me, and I have his number!*

"Okay, I'll come back in a couple hours and try again," I said out loud. "I don't think he knows why I am calling him." I hoped I was right.

Two hours later, two of my friends were helping me paint and refloor my bedroom.

"I just have to swing up to the police station real quick," I told them. "If you have to go before I get back, that's fine. I don't know how long it will take; probably less than an hour." They looked at me curiously.

"Are you okay? Why are you going to the police station?"

"Yeah, I'm fine. I just have to go call my grandpa and get him to admit he abused me on the phone so they have evidence to proceed with the legal process," I said matter-of-factly. "I tried to do it earlier, but he wasn't home, so hopefully he is now and it will just take a few minutes." The two of them looked at me like I was leaving out part of the story, which was true—any emotional part had been buried for the moment.

"I just have to go get it over with. Thanks for your help!" I fled down the stairs.

Back at the desk with Jerk Cop, I told him the number again. Ralph answered this time and told me he just got back from the store. I wanted to smirk at the officer, but I was too nervous about describing memories that were embarrassing and difficult.

I kept asking Ralph, "Do you remember the time this happened?" And following it with as many details as I could without it sounding out of context. I looked away from Jerk Cop while I spoke, then back at him to see if I was doing this right. He kept giving me a thumbs up or would motion his index finger like a wheel turning if he wanted me to keep talking about a subject. Getting gestured feedback from a cop I didn't like while incriminating my grandfather by indirectly sharing the experience of being molested as a child in explicit detail was cringe-worthy.

"Why are you asking me about this stuff?" He sounded barely irritated or maybe suspicious.

"I just feel a little crazy and it helps me to get my memories straight for therapy," I lied. After ten minutes that felt like several hours, we got off the phone.

"I'll call you again soon then," I said as a token of my guilt and caretaking for what I was doing. I noticed my body was closed off. My arms and legs were crossed and my feet sat up on the edge of the chair to ball up my body.

"You did a good job," Jerk Cop said, looking at me, "I think we have enough evidence here. I will make a report and

Larry will go over it before we send it to the District Attorney. I'll walk you out." I followed him down the stairs, again noticing my warrior outfit appearing on my body in my mind's eye. I felt my deerskin cloak hug my shoulders and watched my sealskin boots step down the stairs.

We reached the door and I held out my hand to shake Jerk Cop's as a compromise for the disdain I felt against him for not empathizing with me and the love I felt for him as the only person who went through this re-traumatizing experience with me. He was a jerk, but he had also told me I had done a good job.

I drove home and sat on the new floor of my safe haven, holding my knees to my chest and sobbing out all the fear and guilt that didn't belong in the justice system.

Six months passed before I called Larry to see why I hadn't heard from the DA. He told me it was common for paperwork to be pushed aside or lost. Throughout this process, there were so many times I felt like my story didn't matter. I imagined validating someone's experience of injustice within a system of people processing paperwork that has no emotional weight for them. I wondered if they ever just stopped at their desk and looked at the reports in front of them, imagining the people who had to make them; what they feel, how they walk, what kind of car they drive, the clothes they wear, if they have families, what their favorite movie might be. Do they ask themselves who these papers are as people?

Larry had driven several hours one way with another officer to talk to Ralph. I don't know what that conversation was like, but I know it was validating to find that out. Someone cared enough about who my papers were as a person to go all that way and ask for more information to provide a more complete understanding of what I experienced, perhaps with the intention that the outcome would match what I deserved. He made sure the paperwork was at the DA's and called me back to let me know.

I called the DA every two months for a year to see if they had more information; each time, they said the paperwork hadn't been processed. They prioritized time-sensitive cases, and since I was no longer in danger, mine was not time-sensitive.

The legal process sat static like this for two years. I had moved to Colorado by then and took it upon myself to call Ralph every six months and ask him about his life. If the law was not going to acknowledge that he could be dangerous to other children, someone needed to watch and hold him accountable. Ralph had not admitted having an addiction or needing help. He denied it to me, and while I didn't believe he was seeking opportunities to molest other people, I knew it was a possibility if the right circumstances presented themselves. I also knew that, though he was getting older—almost 90 by then—he still had the opportunity to acknowledge his pain and addiction and to ask for help. If he ever did, I made sure he had been explicitly told and consistently shown that he could come to me and ask where to start. I wasn't calling him to have a relationship; I was calling because the law wasn't picking up the phone.

One afternoon, as I pulled into the parking lot at my apartment in Colorado, my phone rang. The caller ID read

"Alaska State Troopers" and I thought, *Oh no, I hope everyone is okay.*

The person on the other end explained they were calling about the report I had filed over two years earlier. He told me the state would not be pressing charges; they did not believe the court would convict him because it had been so long since he perpetrated. They would not have options for sentencing because they would not want to put someone in jail who was so old.

"I am concerned that he may be harming other kids," I explained; "This is not about retaliation for myself, it is about keeping the community safe. He still has a driver's license and he lives alone."

"I understand. The best thing you can do would be to call The Office of Children's Services and make sure there is a report filed so there is a record of his behavior," he responded.

"I have filed a report," I rebutted; "I know there is a record, but that means someone else would have to file a report and it would have already happened."

"I understand," he repeated. "The state isn't going to press charges on this report. Your only option is to make sure there is a child abuse report filed." I hung up the phone. Any research I did and what he had told me indicated there was nothing else I could do. I didn't want to do anything else. I was too tired to fight a legal battle. If my case had more weight with public organizations or with the elected officials in the state justice system, they may have moved forward. Maybe if there were more incriminating evidence, Ralph would have been arrested and the report would have been stronger. On the phone, he admitted to molesting me twice, but that didn't seem like enough. Maybe I could have painted a more detailed picture for them or gotten more evidence from Ralph. I didn't want to do this anymore, though. Every time I had to recount my story, call Ralph myself to investigate whether he was around children, and now hear that the state wouldn't move forward with my case, I felt invalidated and uncared for. He wasn't listed as a sex offender for anyone to hold him accountable and protect their children. There was absolutely zero accountability for him from the state. His victim was the only person that seemed concerned about this happening to someone else. Perhaps this was because I knew what it felt like. I knew the repercussions of abuse. Did anyone working at the DA's office understand them? Did anyone working in the legal system know the risk they took by leaving a man who had molested a child unaccountable?

I could have asked to talk to another person. I could have called back. I'm sure there are options I didn't understand or know about, but I was tired of fighting and there was nobody there fighting with me. I chose the unfair option of continuing to call Ralph every six months as a poor method of accountability.

I sat in my car in the parking lot, staring at the dashboard for a few minutes, grieving the frustration of victims coming forward and empathizing with those who don't. I could go back and wrack my brain, going over each detail and how I could have done it differently, yet there comes a time when problem-solving mutates into an interrogation, retelling becomes a form of proving it to strangers, and the questioning transforms into the gaslighting I experienced in the process of deciding this was worth my own attention. I didn't want to go through the torment of proving this was worth the attention of the state anymore.

I picked up my phone and made the call. “Hey Ralph, it's Sierra. What have you been up to lately?”

10

"It's much darker when a light goes out than it would have been if it never had shone."
- John Steinbeck

The first time I was given a platform on which to speak about childhood abuse in front of hundreds of people, I felt ready. I imagined standing in the dark with a spotlight on me, alone, on stage, where my purpose was to shatter silence. The warrior in me returned as she had five years earlier when I spoke to my family. I would be facing more people who had experienced abuse and wanted to break the cycle of pain. I knew this was my destiny. However, I had one problem: I was as horrified as I was excited.

I reflected on the years I had worked relentlessly and determinately for this moment, as many before and after me have trained and studied to accomplish significant goals in their lives. As the moment of truth approaches, the doubt and shame begin to creep in. *What if I start crying on stage? What if people are not interested in my story? What if I sound like a victim instead of an empowered and recovered woman? What if people believe I am sick for forgiving and loving a man who hurt me for so long? What if I stutter? What if I succeed?*

The cosmic joke of my life is that I have experienced severe social anxiety, and yet, I love to perform.

The evening before my speaking engagement, I lied down in the event room and closed my eyes. I saw myself onstage in the outfit I had picked out, holding the microphone, walking from one side to the other as I spoke, smiled, laughed, and cried. In my imagination, the room was dark and I felt the spotlight on me as I shared. As if time had stopped, the people in the seats froze and I saw a council of women standing around the perimeter of the room. I saw ancestors, mentors who had passed, and women I did not know. They wore layers of white and boldly stood as if they held in place the room, the building, maybe even the entire universe. It wasn't strenuous. They were gentle and focused as if promptly extracting any fear from my nervous system while I was on stage.

"We will all be here, Sierra. Standing along the walls, holding your hand, and you will know exactly what to say, but if you don't, I will whisper it in your ear," my grandmother promised me. "Open your eyes now and write down these words to read to yourself: *What if I spoke, this is who I am. And that is enough?*" I opened my eyes for a moment, wrote those exact words, and closed my eyes to this mother of wisdom.

She finished, "Now, let go of everything else you have prepared. You don't need it. Your preparation has been your devotion to healing for the past several years, my child."

I set my sights on opening my heart and throat to what needed to be said, and I saw every woman who had brought me into this life standing around the room in circle, singing with me. They held hands and harmonized. Between these wise women appeared all the versions of me through childhood, adolescence, and young adulthood. These versions of myself were adorned in bold reds, oranges, and yellows, representing their courage, confidence, and energy. Bamboo forests, vines, and giant sequoias bloomed behind them; green and wood symbols of hope, groundedness, and growth. In my throat, a small blue flame was born. As I sang, it grew brighter, yet softer, as the loving honesty and truth would emerge the next morning.

A whisper suddenly fell upon my body as my clothing changed into a flowing purple dress: "This is your time, queen." I breathed into the roots, the colors calling all the power and love in the universe to be with me. This journey was about to extend beyond me.

I practiced my speech late that night in the stairwell of the hotel; it was my last chance to perfect each word and moment. I recorded myself to play it as I slept, wiring it into my brain so it would become a part of me. Each time I practiced, I talked past my allotted time. I stumbled over my words. I kept adding things I had never said before.

I thought, *This speech could be multiple books; there is so much content here. How do I summarize this experience in 12 minutes? What if I can't do this? What if I freeze? What if people who believe in me see me fail?*

My preparation was no longer working. Everything I had worked on up to that point became fruitless and ineffective. I was failing. I gave up the practice.

I went to bed with my earbuds in and woke up every hour, my heart racing with panic.

In the morning, I got in the shower and cried. *I could just leave this hotel,* I thought. *I don't have to do this. I can just run and never go back.*

But if I chose to do that, I knew I would regret it forever. If I stayed silent and ran away, I would continue the cycle of silence. This was the time I had worked for. This was the time I was going to dig deep and remember every shred of forgiveness for myself. Every woman who came before me would be standing in that room. I remembered my nieces and my past students. I remembered the women who would come after me. So many women did not have the chance to stand on a stage and say this was their story, too. This had to be for them. This had to be for the three-year-old girl who didn't know how to be heard. I promised her I would do what she couldn't do so long ago. I had to keep this promise.

I stood by the stage, listening to the speaker before me. His themes were inventions and adolescent bullying. I don't remember his speech because it took all my energy to focus on breathing slowly.

The event coordinator approached me and asked, “How much time does he have left?”

“I have no idea. I'm breathing,” I said as a reminder to myself that it was my only job in that moment.

“Do you want me to read your bio or say something else?” He asked.

“I trust you. Say whatever you feel.” I let go of preparation.

“She had a tremendous year in 2017. More than that and even deeper than that, she is all heart, she is all vulnerability, she is all love, she's all sweetness, she's all kindness...and she got a little bit of fierce in there, too. Please welcome to the stage, Sierra Frost!”

That was it. The fierceness. This is where I was coming from. As I stepped onto the stage, the fear melted away. As if every molecule of energy in that room supported my purpose, I spoke gracefully, unapologetically, and with forgiveness. I laughed, I shook, I cried, and I breathed deep. The whole room was in this together, held by my feminine ancestors and fueled by the little girl version of myself standing beside me. She never stopped smiling the entire time. All her pain was melting away as she watched the crowd listen to her through me, taking notes with focused attention.

Twelve minutes were up and my timing was exact. The audience stood up and hollered and applauded, and she danced all over the stage yelling, "Yes!! Yes!! I am free!!"

The ancestors in the room stood tall and strong, nodding in agreement that destiny was here, smiling as they watched the young version of me let loose on the stage. In that moment, nobody in the room mattered more than the little girl that only I and my invisible circle of women could see.

I left the stage, forgetting any of the words I had said, but feeling invincible. The stage was my home, a territory I claimed for 12 minutes, and my speech was the birth of my origin story. All these people witnessed as I delivered the final reclamation of my courage. Still, the most important part of this story was what began to happen 24 hours later.

It was a long workday, and I pulled in late to the parking lot at home. My phone rang and when I saw it was Ralph calling me, I stared at the number for a long moment. He had not called me in 4 years; the last time he had apologized to me. I had written him a letter a month earlier to thank him for briefly asking about my life when I last saw him. I wanted him to know that it was helpful and invite him to do it more, to tell me about his life, and to write letters.

"Hey, Ralph?"

"Hi, yes, this is me. Are you happy? In your life?" He opened deeply and directly. I stayed calm in my excitement while internally I was jumping up and down. It is not an exaggeration to say I had never heard him ask another person how they were doing before.

"Yes, Grandpa, I am happy. Yesterday I did a public speaking event. I was so scared, but I did it and I feel proud. I love working for myself and the work I am doing is so wholehearted, Grandpa. I am happier than I have ever felt before." I had been calling him Ralph for 7 years by then, but that night, Grandpa blurted out of my mouth.

"Oh. Oh, well that sounds great." I knew he didn't know what I did for work, and that was okay. He went on, "Do you have a boyfriend? What happened to the boy you drove to Colorado with? Do you have friends there, too?"

As I sat in the darkness, my eyes widened, my jaw dropped, and I stuttered in shock for a moment. This may sound like a normal conversation to have with a family member, but Ralph did not have the social skills to engage like this, nor had he ever shown the emotional capacity to initiate and continue a conversation about another person without making it about him. This was a continuation of firsts that I had never heard Ralph ask anyone—about specific activities, social encounters, or details of their life experiences. He was behaving several skill levels higher than ever before. In my gut was a sense of magic that somehow my speech had been delivered to him through methods beyond my comprehension of the divine. During this phone call, I sincerely considered whether I controlled the universe.

"Yeah, Kent. I don't see him anymore. I hope he is well. I

don't have a boyfriend and that's okay with me. I do have some really great friends and two roommates who are extremely supportive. Our home is full of love and music. I have a great community of people," I spoke slowly with conviction and loudly so he could hear me.

"I'm glad you have these people. It's good that boy is doing well." My grandparents had always been comforted by me having men in my life and it used to irritate me. That day, I was grateful he asked and knew I was well.

"Anyway, I wanted to ask you if I can send you a check in the mail. I'm going to die soon and I don't know what will happen with the house or anything. I want you to have money like I have said and I don't know if anyone will give it to you after I die." He was very flat as he talked about the end of his life. I remembered how he had told me he would give me money when he died each time he apologized for abusing me. Gift-giving was the only form of love he knew how to use to try and correct his actions. While money was not my love language, what he was offering meant much more to him. He was taking action to follow through on the promise he had included in his apologies for years.

I responded with the same neutral tone. "Is that what you want? To die?"

"Yeah. I haven't left the house in two months and nobody visits me except your uncle once in a while. I can't garden anymore and my body hurts to move. I just have my cat. I'm going to die in the spring. I want to give you money first. I can't write because my hand is too shaky, so I think your uncle would help me write the address," he said, planning out loud to me.

"Ok." I couldn't focus on the money. "Did you get my letter last month?"

"Yes, I got it. I have your address from it. I can't write back because my hand is too shaky. I will send the money next week," he said, continuing to focus on the money.

"Ok. If you're going to die, is there anything you want us to talk about that we haven't yet? Anything you want to say before it's too late?" This was surprisingly comfortable to ask him, but because we had been so uncomfortable with each other before, it felt as though we could never exceed the discomfort of those previous conversations.

"No, I don't think we need to talk. I think the family wants to put me in a home. They whisper when I am in the room so I can't hear them. They do not like me. I will die in the spring," he repeated, and I knew some of what he was saying was true. I considered the duality of the natural consequences for what Ralph had done and the disintegrity of treating someone as less than human, no matter what horrific mistakes they had made.

"I would like to tell you some things, Grandpa," I said effortlessly. I had developed the confidence to ask for what I wanted and say what I thought. "I want to thank you for having difficult conversations with me many times about abuse and my childhood. It has been very important to me as an adult. I know these conversations are not easy to have and I believe you are brave for having them with me anyway. I am grateful that you have asked me about my life today and when you ask me those questions I feel cared for by you. Lastly, I'm glad you are still in my life. It has helped me to grow and be more of who I am. Would you like it if I could try and visit you before you die in the spring?" As these words spilled out of my mouth unplanned, I knew I had never felt so sure of my dedication to inviting Ralph into my life over the years. While I was always committed to giving him the option, I never believed he would show up as he had that night. I wondered if the things I had learned with Ralph were finally outweighing the pain he had caused.

His tone conveyed his shock as if to say, *You want to come here to visit me?* "Yes, I would like you to visit again if I send you enough money to do that," he answered, following with, "I think you should use the money to invest in your business. You should do whatever makes you happiest with it, but it sounds like your business is really successful and makes you happy."

I wondered if I could ever explain to him what I do for work. I felt the circle of forgiveness coming to completion through his intentions. He wanted to invest in the work I had chosen as a direct result of his abusive actions. In that moment, I felt I was the luckiest person in the world to experience this journey. This was the gift of adversity. This was the moment I realized there is nothing more important than to keep believing in the good of people, no matter how many mistakes they have made or how deeply they have hurt us.

"Ok Grandpa," I smiled tearily, "I will use it for my business. Thank you for supporting me."

"Nobody else will talk to me," he said, indirectly telling me about his pain. "Your parents don't talk to me; I ask how your dad is, but I don't get a response from anyone." I want him to ask me directly, but I know he has practiced this habitual passivity for many years.

"Well, we fished together last summer and had a blast. I think he is doing really well. He is such an amazing teacher and we have a lot of fun when we get to spend time together. Cody seems well, also. He is volunteering in his community and working at night. The girls are getting really big and they are active. Mom is doing yoga and seems to love it. They are all happy, too, Grandpa."

"Oh." He stopped short for a moment and held his breath as if to acknowledge the punishment of losing his family. "I'm glad they are happy."

What he did not say out loud was that he was not. The intensity of the regret he was living with would make death a sweet escape from daily remembrances that his actions had cost him the family he thought he had cared for better than his dad had cared for him. Perhaps he had done better than his dad, but it didn't result in what he seemed to have wanted. He knew he had made the wrong choices in hopes of keeping them around, and now it was their choice not to share their lives with him. He knew he was to blame.

He called again two days later to say he was going to mail the check, but he hung up abruptly. I wondered if my aunt and uncle had returned. They stayed with him when they were in town and had been helping him clear the house of unwanted artifacts from hoarding. He seemed paranoid. He did not want anyone to know he was giving me money.

Ralph sent the check and I bought a plane ticket to visit in March. We sat on the couch and he told me about the physical pain of aging while his cat sat on his lap. He reminded me that he would die soon. I never gave him pity, but I always validated his feelings.

“That sounds intense, painful, and sad to not be able to garden anymore,” I responded. “How do you feel about knowing you will die?”

“I want to die. I am ready. The doctor said my pacemaker battery is going to go out in May. Don't tell anyone that, though, they don't know.” My aunt told me the same thing the next day, illustrating the mistrust and hurt that ran deep in my family. “I don't want to live in a home, so I think I will just die when that happens.”

“Oh, does death feel easier to accept, knowing there is a timeline like that?” I suggested, offering some more emotional language to understand what he was experiencing.

“Yes. I can't do everything I want to anymore, so I just make toast for breakfast, take my pills, and some days I can get dressed and other days I just stay in my robe,” he said, speaking with a faraway stare. “It's no way to live. I can't take care of myself and nobody else will do that. I am lonely and sad.” I watched him curiously as he labeled his emotions. He was accepting the reality of being alone at the end of his life.

“And you don't want to go to a home where people would take care of you?” I asked, pointing to the possibility of community.

“No,” he asserted, “I don't want to leave my house. If I get worse and have to go to a home, I will kill myself.”

“Oh, I hear that. I know your house is important to you. Do you have a plan to kill yourself?”

“Yes, I have some pills and I can just take all of those,” he answered sternly, as if to prove he would do it.

“Ok, well, I can imagine wanting to die while feeling

sadness and loneliness." I was not going to tell him not to do it. I could see his pain and I had wanted to die for much of my life; who was I to say whether continuing his life would be healthy for him?

"So, I have done everything I need to do to die," he continued. "I gave you money and there is a will, so everyone can have money. The only other thing to do would be to talk to your dad."

"Are you going to do that?"

"He won't talk to me!" Ralph slightly raised his voice in frustration. "I don't know how to talk to him. I don't know what to say that he would want to talk to me. I'm dead to him already." I looked at him empathetically. He was right. I didn't know if there was anything he could have said that would speak louder than the decades of actions that couldn't be revoked. If there were words, Ralph didn't have them, and while he knew that, he didn't believe that finding the words was possible, nor did he know how to ask for help with that. I watched his stare travel far away from the couch we sat on. He had one thing to do before he died and he didn't know how to do it. He did not know how to care for his son. Maybe not talking to him was the only way to care for him anymore. I could not offer to help him with his words because they needed to be his own, so we sat in a brief silence, sharing the feeling of too little, too late.

"Grandpa, would you like to see some photos of where I live? I have lots on my phone I would like to show you," I said, bringing him back to the living room.

"Mmhmm," he grunted, looking at my phone. "It's just amazing that you can have photos on that tiny thing!"

"I know! It's so much different than when you were

taking photos of your vacations with film! Look, we can take a photo of us right now, even," I opened my camera and turned the view so he could see us on the screen.

"Oh, look at that!" Ralph started to smile and then giggle as I made excited faces and snapped a dozen selfies of us together. These are some of the only photos of Ralph smiling that I have seen. Even in his teenage photos, his expressions seem stoic.

I showed him photos of hikes, landscapes, and my friends, and I told him short stories. He asked for some repeats when he couldn't hear and otherwise gave quiet mumbles of affirmation. Without planning, the roll flipped to a photo of me and my parents.

Ralph's eyes widened. "Is that your dad?!"

"Yes! We took a trip to Seattle together in January. We had so much fun—I can show you these photos, too. Does he look old to you?"

"No, he looks like he did when he was sixteen! He's young! And so is Michelle." His face was not smiling, but his voice sounded as if he were. "Huh. They look pretty good." I continued to show him photos of our trip and tell him stories about how much fun we had together. After some time, he started to tear up silently.

During this visit, Ralph had talked about sadness, loneliness, and frustration. He had laughed and welled up. This was an emotional man I had never met. Later, my aunt commented that the man she saw interact with me was not the man she knew. My family knew that Ralph was different when he spoke to me, and while they didn't know how this happened and didn't understand it, they supported that I cared for him and that we had a unique relationship. I was pleased they saw what I had experienced in the last few years of his life.

Ralph lived over two years past the estimated death date of his pacemaker. He never went to a home. One day, some family friends went to check on him and found him in a coma on the floor. After a day in the hospital, his organs began to fail and he was granted the death he had wanted for years. He was almost 96. Until then, he had remained healthy enough to care for himself and his cat. He'd only stopped gardening three years prior.

My aunt visited twice during the day he spent in a coma, but Ralph died alone. He had outlined his own obituary, filed all the paperwork for his will, and requested to be cremated. He died in August—the same month he had stopped abusing me, the same month I had told the family he had abused me, and the same month his wife had died. August was the height of the harvest from his garden each year and marked for me each milestone in our story.

I went to Ralph's home a few days after he passed. I sat in his room and looked at photos of his family and his youth. On the orange 1970s shag carpet, I spoke to him about all the emotions I felt: deep sadness that I couldn't share my life with him and that he wouldn't be asking me questions anymore, relief for him that his unhealthy and unhappy life had ended, curiosity as to whether he had killed himself or if his pacemaker had finally given out, anger that the majority of our relationship had been heartbreaking trauma and severe pain, and deep loneliness because the person who went through the entire timeline of that trauma with me was gone. I wondered who I was now that our relationship on Earth had ended. It had informed so much of my passion for working in the field of recovery; I had spent years of energy avoiding and then healing it, and it highlighted how courageous, loving, and resilient I was.

My family did not hold a memorial. There were waves of apathy and confusing emotions of love, or wanting to feel love in place of emptiness. Many of my family members were glad he was gone and had grieved his loss years before when they stopped talking to him.

I wanted to celebrate our relationship. I wanted to be sad with my community because I had lost someone I cared for. There was a disconnect when I told people my grandpa had died—it wasn't the whole story. It wasn't a *regular* grandfather’s death. I didn't want to explain or justify our relationship, either.

My entire childhood had involved suffering alone, and I could not choose that for myself, this time—nor did I need to. I chose a Sunday and invited my local friends to come by my house in Alaska at their convenience. We took some nature walks and played with the plants; I created a mandala with seeds, berries, and leaves I had found to honor his life; and they listened to me cry. Some of them painted pictures for me, wrote me letters, or sang to me.

I took some photos of Ralph along with a statue of a standing happy Buddha from his room when I left. The last letter I had written to him said I was writing a book about our lives separately and together. I told him it would be a tale of resilience and unconditional love. I asked him if he wanted me to include any specific stories and what he thought I should write about. The book would be released on his birthday, the gift of sharing our story with the world. We never got to talk about it—by then, he could not write back to me, and he stopped answering the phone—probably because he couldn't hear well enough. I wrote that I was grateful he was my grandfather and I was glad he was in my life. I reminded him that I loved him.

While I sat staring at the container of ashes I'd accidentally found, my little girl self entered Ralph's room and sat next to me. She watched as I stared and sobbed at his name on the label of the tin.

"I feel sad, too?" She said as if asking permission.

"Yeah," I confirmed, "it's okay to feel sad. It's okay to feel anything."

"Well," she smiled, "I liked having a grandpa the last couple years."

"What do you mean?"

"You know, how he started asking questions and you stopped calling him Ralph." She put her tiny hand in mine. "You called him Grandpa again. You shared stories together and he even laughed that one time when you took a selfie together on your phone. I liked that—having a grandpa." I was bawling as I took out my phone. I pulled her into my lap and wrapped my arms around her while we looked at the photo together. We were both crying and laughing together.

"It's really special that we got to have a grandpa for over two years," I said to her. "He showed up. It took a long time, but he showed up and he loved us. That's why I started calling him Grandpa again. I want you to know that these last years were just as real as all the painful ones before that, ok?"

"Good. They were my favorite years with him." She

stood up and started rummaging through photos and piles, standing on boxes to see the top shelves.

"Mine too," I agreed, still sobbing.

"Hey, look out the window! All those people are back!" My four-year-old self pointed excitedly. I stood up and looked outside. I first saw my ancestors: my mother's parents whom I never met, entire camps of Native Americans, generations of farmers from Illinois, Navy sailors from the California coast, merchant Marines and working-class Canadians, and Anglo-Saxons of England. After them were characters of strength such as Joan of Arc, Mother Teresa, Gandhi, Nelson Mandela, John Lennon, Baroness Bertha von Suttner, and Jesus. Behind them were endurers of violence including the Rotherham children, Dr. Martin Luther King Jr. and the boys and girls of the Birmingham Children's Crusade, victims of The Great Leap Forward, and the billion women who are sexually assaulted worldwide each year.

They extended from the Spenard municipality to all of Anchorage, spilling into the Matsu Valley, down the Kenai Peninsula, and lining the coast as they held time still. Each member was unwavering. They felt the earth under their rooted feet and pulled fortitude from beneath that extended as robust rays into the sky. They held their palms toward each other, communicating that they would hold this space together and for each other in a network of energy.

I watched as, one by one, they stood down, took a knee, and bowed their heads in a wave of relief and honor.

"What are they doing?" Little Sierra asked.

"I think the treaty agreements have all been fulfilled," I said. "The warriors are now protected."

"What?" She didn't understand.

"Everybody won—you, me, and Grandpa."

"Yes!" She clenched her fists and pulled them down toward her shoulders in victory. "We should have some cake to celebrate!"

"We should," I replied; "let's have it on his birthday. We'll have cake and a new book." My four-year-old self wrapped her arms around my neck and hugged me tight. I rocked her from side to side as the alpenglow out the window set the land into silhouette.

"Let everything happen to you: beauty and terror.
Just keep going."
-Rainer Maria Rilke

So, What?: The Invitation

My story is important, but even more important is the response to the question, "So, what? Why does this matter to me?" There are many answers. It matters because you want to be free of some past pain that lives in your thoughts, emotions, or body—pain you may or may not have memories of. It matters because you know people who have experienced abuse and/or mental illness and you want to help them. It matters because you know there is more to life, but you aren't sure what that is. Some things you may be missing without knowing is connection to other people (yes, even if you have family and friends around you), creative expression, or work that aligns with your values and goals.

Here are some things to remember: you know a lot of people who have experienced interpersonal trauma, mental illness, and isolation. They may tell you about it or they may not, but regardless of your knowledge of it, it is there. Your family members have experienced trauma, and it is passed down through your DNA.[1] You are biologically wired to connect with other people to tell stories, to hear stories, and to belong. If your life does not include human connection and creativity, you probably feel like something is missing.

Whether or not you know what is missing, there is a trap that humans fall for: asking ourselves, "What's wrong with

---

[1] Rachel Yehuda et al., *Phenomenology and Psychobiology of the Intergenerational Response to Trauma,*(Massachusetts, Springer, 1998)

me?”

When we are hurt and abandoned, we think it is a reflection of our own character and that we are undeserving of care and connection. We see other people who appear happy with their families, jobs, college degrees, and marriages, and we think they are fulfilled and that we must be at fault for feeling like we aren't. Believing there is something fundamentally wrong with us causes us to live as if paralyzed. Shame is an experience so threatening to our safety that we run, hide, fight, and numb ourselves to avoid feeling it. One of the fastest, most accessible, and most socially-acceptable ways to escape shame is to externally alter our state.

We escape and create addictions. Addiction looks like excessively drinking, using drugs, eating, fasting, exercising, shopping; engaging in relationships that aren't healthy; or even feeling emotions in cycles–anxiety, depression, panic, mania, and more. These are all used to escape or numb feelings that are deeply uncomfortable to us. We feel unsafe and we use any of these tools to fight, flee, or dissociate from our bodies, also known as freezing.

These coping mechanisms bump up our endorphins and hormones, relieving us from the pain of stress, regardless of the cause. This cycle really works! The problem is, our bodies become addicted to the chemical spikes and we stop producing our own endorphins to stay balanced because we learn that we are going to receive those endorphins from an outside source. This dependence can happen quickly or develop over time based on many factors such as genetic disposition, environment, previous experience, and more. It often feels sudden when we experience it firsthand—like you woke up one day with a full-blown addiction—because it can be hard to notice the gradual steps that led you there.

Though addiction is modeled and even encouraged in our culture through drinking alcohol, getting high, buying material things, and eating at most social occasions, realizing we are experiencing an addiction commonly feels shameful. Shame is the most powerful emotion preventing us from believing we are capable and deserving of change.[2] Shame makes it easy for us to unconsciously hide, and we avoid sharing the experience with others. We self-sabotage, we shut down, and we isolate. We avoid the very cure to shame, which is healthy connection with other people.

Many of us tend to process everything intellectually—as if we can think ourselves out of any situation if we are logical enough. The problem with this strategy is that cognitive experiences are processed in our brains, but emotional experiences are processed in our bodies.[3] We often disconnect from our bodies to escape our emotions; we breathe shallow, we clench our jaws, we hold our shoulders tightly up to our ears, or we hunch over. We experience chronic pain that may be temporarily relieved through physical methods like chiropractic adjustment, massage therapy, Rolfing, and more, but those improvements will only be sustainable if we are also treating the emotional source in our bodies. Similarly, we often try to process our emotions cognitively using talk therapy, but this is

---

[2] Brené Brown, *Daring Greatly: How the Courage to be Vulnerable Transforms the Way We Live, Love, Parent, and Lead,* (New York, Gotham Books, 2012).
[3] Lauri Nummenmaa, et al., *Bodily Maps of Emotions, (*Proceedings of the National Academy of Sciences, 2014), 646-651.

also incomplete.[4] Because we experience trauma with our minds and our bodies, we must use both to process our experiences if we are to recover completely. Despite cultural language that speaks of each piece individually, we have to stop separating our bodies, minds, and spirits and see ourselves as one integrated whole if we want to revolutionize healthcare.

The common cycle of our culture avoids emotions, fosters addictions, disconnects us from our bodies, and isolates us from each other, creating the perfect storm that allows trauma to control our lives for years, decades, and often lifetimes. I invite you to bravely and radically step out of the status quo of our culture. I invite you to feel, be present in your body, and connect with other people who are authentic in the human experience. If you feel alone or disallowed to be so revolutionary, accept me as your comrade and this book as your permission slip. It is time.

---

[4] Bessel A. Van der Kolk, *The Body Keeps the Score: Brain, Mind, and Body in the Healing of Trauma,* (New York, Viking, 2014).

The Invitation: Processing Emotions

The Info

Researchers describe emotions as the "cement that unites the body and brain," and peptides explain this phenomenon. Peptides are molecular chains of amino acids smaller than protein chains. They are created by chemical bonds between molecules in the body. We call these chains hormones and neuropeptides such as estrogen, testosterone, dopamine, serotonin, or cortisol. Our bodies naturally produce a certain amount of these chemicals or we supplement them externally in the form of pharmaceutical medications from health professionals.

Peptides move through our bodies via neural pathways, the circulatory system, and respiratory passages. They affect how we behave: urges to agree/disagree, drink/urinate, fight/flee, etc.[5] Emotions direct us in what we do and when we do it. For example, if I see a person who looks like someone who has hurt me before, I may feel fear; that fear may dictate that I run from that person or act aggressively towards them. Because the brain cannot tell the difference between perception and reality, fear rises whether the person *has* hurt me before or simply *looks like* someone who has. Whether I am aware that I feel fearful or not, the emotion impacts how I behave.[6]

At a cellular level, peptides attach to receptors on cells and affect the new cell's reactions. Peptides can permeate a cell

---

[5] Cheryl A. MacDonald, "The Biology of Emotions." *Health Psychology Center*, (California, Health Psychology of San Diego, 2015).
[6] Keith J. Karren, et al., *Mind/Body Health: The Effects of Attitudes, Emotions, and Relationships*, 5th ed., (Utah, Pearson, 2013).

membrane. When this happens in a large group of cells, it can intensely influence our emotional state. Peptides can communicate in a variety of ways and in different areas depending on the type and amount of peptides present.

Much of our stress is related to maladaptive responses. For example, if we forget winter is coming and do not leave the house soon enough to defrost our windshield, we arrive late to work. We feel angry, frustrated, or shameful and our coworkers or clients may be upset. This delivers physiological consequences such as clotting factors in our blood, raised cholesterol levels, lowered immune function, tensed muscles, increased blood pressure, and more.[7] This intensity of response to a frosted windshield is not appropriate unless we are going to give medical response and our tardiness could be lethal. Over time, these emotional events create disease in our bodies and can damage our brains if left unprocessed. This is how stress—especially chronic stress—decreases our quality of life physically, emotionally, and cognitively.

The Experience

Label, Locate, Integrate

Your job in this exercise is to drop out of judgment and into self-compassion; curiosity, observation, and connection. Emotions are neutral messengers—positive or negative connotations are judgments we make about them. Throughout this process, tune into any sensations that are changing, moving, or evolving. This is the physical and energetic experience of your emotional process.

---

[7] Bessel, *The Body Keeps the Score.*

This is easiest to do while lying or sitting down in a quiet space where you can close your eyes and relax. Notice the feeling of the surface beneath you. Allow your body to relax into this space and focus on your breathing. As your body relaxes, your breathing may begin to slow and deepen naturally.

1. **Label:** what emotion are you feeling? Is there any deeper or more precise emotion?

2. **Locate:** where in your body do you feel this? What does the sensation feel similar to? What qualities does the it have (weight, color, movement, shape, texture, etc.)?

3. **Integrate:** Validate the emotion(s) and recognize it is okay to have them. Thank them for being with you.

Ask the emotion(s):

- What message do you have for me?
- What is your job?
- What are you most afraid of?
- What are you most proud of?
- What's the most important thing to you?
- Any other questions you to want to ask
- Give the emotion(s) any information they may not have had when they were created—experiences you had after that time and resources you have in your life now, such as people, places, skills, beliefs, etc.

When it feels like your conversation has come to a close, thank your body and emotion for communicating and being part of your life. Let it know it can ask to speak to you again whenever it wants and say goodbye in whatever way makes sense for you.

Reflect with a journal what you learned during this exercise. How does your body feel now? What is different from before you began?

The Point

Emotions are neutral; when we judge them as bad or separate from us, we allow shame to take over and paralyze us. Instead, we can use our emotions as messengers to find out what we want and how best to move forward in life. We use the body as a vessel to harvest the wisdom emotions hold.

The Invitation: Forgiveness

The Info

Research shows that engaging a third-person perspective increases our ability to forgive.[8] We can pull ourselves out of the first-person emotional experience and look at the situation as if it were a movie or a story we were observing. The same areas of the brain used to employ this perspective are used to practice empathy. We engage in forgiveness similarly; this part of the brain explores a personality when we focus on what experiences and circumstances might have led to the person's behavior instead of on the behavior alone.

When we are able to forgive, we are less likely to behave aggressively or become anti-social, as we no longer ruminate over the pain that haunts us over longer periods of time.

The Experience

Forgiveness Perspective Visualization

You will have an easier time embracing this visualization with your eyes closed, but you can choose any relaxed position where you can focus in your imagination. Allow your body to relax and melt into the surface you are on. Gently wiggle any places that are holding extra tension, then inhale normally and exhale fully.

Shift your focus to your imagination and recall the situation you want to forgive with the person who hurt you. Once you are there, take the position of an observer, as if you

---

[8] Emiliano Ricciardi et al., *How the Brain Heals Emotional Wounds: The Functional Neuroanatomy of Forgiveness,* (Maryland, Frontiers in Human Neuroscience, 2013).

were watching a movie scene.

Hit pause and freeze the frame. Focus on the person you want to forgive and allow everything else in the scene to fade out. Observe the person as a character from a movie you are watching for the first time. Notice their clothing, posture, facial expression, and any other details that attract your attention. These things carry little meaning, but practice seeing what is present in the moment without any judgment.

Imagine you could rewind this movie and see the person in a scene of their history. Perhaps you can find an experience they had which would lead to the future scene. Watch them in this learning experience. Notice them objectively as you observe their story.

When you feel that scene resolve, rewind the movie even further to see them newly born. See their family, their medical team, and most importantly, notice their tiny body as a baby swaddled in a blanket. Notice their innocence, purity, and newness to being human. Spend as much time as you want embracing this fresh life who has yet to experience anything.

When you are ready, fast-forward the movie to see significant moments in that person's life as you get a quick summary of what led them to the memory you want to forgive. Now that you have a more comprehensive picture of the person instead of only the behavior that hurt you, imagine your present self walking into the scene. Communicate empathy as it feels right to you and state that you forgive this person. You may want to ask for what you want in the future (even if that is not to spend time with them again), but focus on seeing them as a person and forgiving them.

Allow your present self to walk out of the scene with

your past self so you are safe. As you watch the person receiving your forgiveness, slowly allow your imaginative vision to float up out of the scene. Notice your breath and the surface beneath you once again, stretch, and begin to come back into your body and into the present moment.

Reflect with a journal what you learned during this exercise. Notice any changes you feel or things you learned from this experience. Check in with yourself in the following days and notice any changes in your attachment to this memory or forgiveness since before you started. How does your body feel now? What is different from before you began?

The Point

Forgiveness is often confused with acceptance or passivity. I want to be clear—empathy and perspective do not equal permission for a person to treat you in a way that crosses your boundaries or makes you unsafe.

Forgiveness decreases your personal pain, disease created over time by harbored resentment, and the likelihood of behaving in a retaliating way that has negative consequences for you and others.

You can forgive someone without communicating with them again if you choose. It's all about you.

The Invitation: Move It Through

The Info

Many of us—if not all of us—have experiences where we feel endangered and enter into a sympathetic nervous system state, often called the fight-or-flight response. When we are overwhelmed, we can enter into collapsed immobility, also known as freeze, which is like pausing our fight-or-flight response.[9] Imagine an animal playing dead because fighting or fleeing will not likely be successful; we enter into a desperate plan C.

Freezing could look like fainting, feeling weak, or blacking out. If we stay conscious, we often repress memories of these experiences. When humans freeze, we disallow trauma to move through and out of our bodies and instead hold the experience in our connective tissues. This may present immediately or over time in the form of chronic pain, disability, disease, over-protection of that area of our bodies, or dissociation from the area and/or emotion related to the experience. Typically, the emotion we feel when this happens is the emotion we will feel when it is released—if I am panicking when I store it, I will feel panic when I release it. In other words, we shut down our natural trauma process and instead store the pain inside our bodies.

When animals do this, there is a transition period before they come back to consciousness. During this transition, they shake their bodies. The only animals we know of that don't do this are humans and domesticated animals, such as some dogs

---

[9] Kasia Kozlowska et al., *Fear and the Defense Cascade: Clinical Implications and Management,* (Maryland, U.S. National Library of Medicine, 2015).

or zoo animals. This movement after traumatic events is why wild animals do not hold trauma in their bodies long-term the way humans do. The natural expression of our emotions is often socially unacceptable, but it is essential to our health. Animals who use this shake method do not show the same unhealthy impacts, behavior changes, or long-term health declines that we humans experience.[10]

In short, "shake it off" is scientifically-backed advice for dealing with overwhelming emotions.

The Experience

Shaking Body Scan

Find a spot to sit or lie down and get as comfortable as you can. As you relax, notice how your body feels today. There's no wrong way to feel right now; simply drop into your body with curiosity. As you become aware of your internal self, notice how you are breathing. When you connect with your breath, you notice your body starting to relax. Slowly shift your focus to your left foot. Notice your big toe, your middle toes, and the bottom of your feet. Notice your heel. Notice the top of your foot and how the skin wraps around your ankle.

Brace yourself and lift your foot. Start to wiggle it and explore what it's like to add movement. Go ahead and shake your foot out. You can shake it up and down or right to left. You can move your ankle around in a circle and back the other direction. When you feel completely shaken out, go ahead and put your foot back down.

---

[10] Peter A. Levine, *Waking the Tiger: Healing Trauma,* (California, North Atlantic Books, 1997).

Shift your focus to your right foot. Allow yourself to explore in the same way you noticed your your big toe, your toenail, and the line of toes. Again, feel the bottom pads of your foot in the ankle; feel your heal and the top of your foot. Then lift your right foot and start to scrunch it up, wiggle it, stretch it, and when you are ready, shake it out. When you feel completely shaken out, come back to notice your calves. Feel your shin bones. Feel the tiny muscles on the front of your legs and the big strong muscles on the backs of your calves.

Allow your focus to move up to your knees and notice that—even though your knees are pretty bony—there is some softness there. Feel how the muscles cross and attach the thigh to the crus. Slowly move your attention up to your thighs as if there's a light swirling around them and up toward your hips. Notice the backs, the fronts, the inside, and the outside.

Once you have a heightened awareness of everything about your legs, put your feet flat on the floor and start to move your knees in and out, together and apart to shake out your legs. You can lift your feet and act out a running motion in the air or even a dance.

When your legs feel completely shaken out, shift your focus into your hips. Notice the shape of your hips. Notice how they feel against the surface beneath you. Notice how you can shift your left hip up, then down; your right hip up, then down.

Continue into your lower belly and notice how it's connected to your reproductive organs, to your hips, and to your lower back. Imagine you were a belly dancer, moving only your stomach with all its tiny muscles from one side to the other. They move and crunch, bringing your chest toward your knees and back down. They twist you around one direction and back the other way. Begin to wiggle your hips, then move gradually faster into a shake. If you want, you can even force a bit of laughter to shake your belly out.

When your belly feels completely shaken out, shift your focus through your rib cage into your chest; feel your lungs fill with air and empty again. Recognize your torso in parts; first the front, then the left side, the back, and the right side. Notice that your heart is beating; see if you can feel it now. Notice the place where your arms are attached to your shoulders; roll them backwards and forwards together. Notice how you can roll your right shoulder independently and your left shoulder independently. Wiggle your shoulders up towards your ears and back down towards your hips; up towards your ears and back down towards your hips. Continue that shrugging motion until your shoulders feel completely shaken out.

Notice your upper arms, again spiraling around the backs, the sides, the fronts. Notice your armpits. Notice your elbows and how they help you bend and reach. Notice your forearms. Notice the lengths of your forearms, the hairs on your skin, the fronts, the sides, and the backs of your arms, all the way down to your wrists.

Notice all the tiny bones that make up your wrists and all the ways you can move them. Notice the palms of your hands and the big thumb pad you have. Notice each finger, the length of it, and how much movement you have in it. Notice the backs of your hands, your knuckles, and your fingernails. Put your hands on a surface beneath you and move your elbows like you have chicken wings; when you're ready, allow your hands to move along with you. Shake out your arms until you feel complete, then allow them to rest again.

Notice the length of your neck from your chest, from your shoulders, and from your tall spine. Notice how your jaw and skull sit atop it. Notice your eyebrows, your eye sockets, your cheekbones, your nose, your mouth, your tongue, and your teeth. Notice your ears and see if you can feel the hair on top of your head. Start shaking your jaw and moving around as if you're talking silently. Allow your head to follow, moving it gently from side to side and up and down.

As your exercise reaches toward completion, enjoy shaking your entire body out as much as you can, starting slow and speeding up. Change your speed until you feel like everything has been completely shaken out.

As you finish, focus your awareness one more time inside your body. Feel the surface you're on, then exhale all the way, emptying your lungs even further. Inhale deeply and notice any sensations that are different from those you felt at the beginning of this exercise.

Alternative Experience:

Turn on your favorite upbeat song (or three) and get down, shaking your body as you dance.

The Point

The more we experience events that cause us to freeze, the stronger that freeze response takes hold of our brains and bodies and the more likely we are to respond this way in the future. We can release emotional triggers stored in our bodies by shaking. Some people relate this to fighting or fleeing after the fact, acting it out in our bodies to complete the response.

The Invitation: Use Your Imagination

The Info

Your brain can't tell the difference between perception and reality. Our brain's response to imaginary or perceived triggers is the same as its response to stress triggers in reality. In one study at UC Boulder, participants were taught to associate the pain of a small electric shock to a specific noise.[11] Once brain scans showed this association had been made, the shock experience was removed and participants were split into three groups: one continued to hear the noise out loud, one imagined the noise, and one imagined calming sounds such as birdsongs or rain. The group that heard the noise in reality and the group that imagined it were able to unlearn the association between the noise and the shock. They were able to change their fear response by experiencing the trigger without the pain, whether this was in reality or in their imagination. In other words, they didn't need to put themselves in real danger to change their stress response; instead, they could do so in the safety of their imagination. Beyond that, the researchers noted that the group using their imagination rather than the actual sound had even *more* change in their brain activity, suggesting that our imaginations change our stress responses even more effectively than reality does. The group that avoided thinking of the dangerous noise and instead imagined calming sounds was not able to unlearn their stress response. Their brain scans showed that the fear response to the original sound remained. This debunks the idea that simply focusing on positive thoughts

---

[11] UC Boulder, *Your Brain on Imagination: It's a Lot Like Reality, Study Shows,* (Colorado, ScienceDaily, 2018).

can lower our long-term stress. It may lower our stress temporarily when we aren't experiencing triggers, but as soon as we hear the sound, see the person, or smell the scent that triggers stress, we will see the same neurological response and unhealthful impacts.

Keep this in mind: if the brain is unlearning stress through imagination, the cascade of stress-related health problems also resolves. To be clear, if you imagine the same painful memory over and over with the same stressful overtones, you will continue to experience stress as if you are reliving that event. I am not encouraging you to think of the same memory as it played out in the past. I am encouraging you to use your creativity and imagination to rewrite your memories into a story that serves you better.

Remember, everyone is different; depending on the strength of a trigger, this may take more than one attempt to rewire. Factors such as how long we have been ruminating over the memory, how intense the experience was, how many times we experienced a similar trigger, and others will change the relief process for each individual. I highly recommend including a professional when practicing this technique, especially if you feel overwhelmed or stuck.

The Experience

Part 1—Journal to Create Your Goal

1. **Make this is a positive statement.** Write what you want, not what you want to avoid. If what comes to mind is something you want to stop, simply flip it.

Example: *From, "I want to stop having recurring dreams of trauma" to, "I want to sleep through the night and feel well-rested."*

2. **Show how this is within your control.**

Example: *I can go to bed at the same time each night. I can read a positive story or listen to positive music before I go to bed, and I can hire a coach who works with trauma to help me with the things I may not know how to resolve on my own.*

3. **Be specific.** Add details to define or clarify how and when you will do this.

Example: *Right now, I am having recurring dreams six nights a week. By May, I will have no more than 3 recurring dreams in a month.*

4. **Describe your goal using your senses.** When you reach it, what will you see, feel, hear, or smell?

Example: *I will feel energized when I wake in the morning from a still and uninterrupted night's sleep. I will see myself in the mirror and smile with gratitude as I hear the shower water start flowing and smell my shampoo.*

5. **Break your goal up into manageable pieces.** What do the steps to this goal look like?

Example: *I will go to bed at 10pm M-F. I will choose 3 positive* *affirmations to read before bed at 9:45pm. I will hire a coach by the end of Tuesday. I will decrease my recurring dreams by one night each week.*

6. **Make a list of the resources you have and the ones you will need.**

Example: *I can set a bedtime alarm at 9:15 in my phone. I have affirmation cards at home or I can write new ones. I need a coach and a way to track how many recurring dreams I am having. I need to determine how energetic I feel each morning.*

7. **Specify how you will know your goal has been achieved.** How will you measure this? Use lots of imagery so you can identify it well.

Example: *I will look at my tracking sheet and see only three nights marked with a recurring dream in one month. I will feel energized when I wake up. I will smile and know I can do anything. I will share with my coach that we can make a new goal. I will feel excited to get rest at night. I may even see improved work performance or start going to yoga again with my renewed energy.*

8. **Check your consequences.** They could feel good or bad. How does this change affect other people or areas in your life? What incentives might urge you not to change? Who might you want to tell about your goal?

Example: *I may want to do new activities that seem weird to* *my family or friends. I may feel more capable or brave and believe more in miracles. If I don't change, I have permission to stay up late and watch funny television shows. I have an excuse to be tired and not do my best during the day. I have an excuse to relax at night when I am tired. I may need to give myself permission to relax and to risk doing my best even if I make mistakes. I may want to tell my partner I am going to go to bed at a certain time from now on so I can work on this goal.*

You can now write your complete goal.

Example: *I will have no more than 3 recurring dreams per month by May 1st.*
I have these resources: ______________________________.
I will need to get these resources:

______________________________________.

*I can work through these consequences:*______________________________.
*I am excited for these consequences:*__________________________________.
I may let these people know I will be making this change:

______________________________.

Part 2—Drop the Goal

Now that you have done the journaling exercise, go back to number 7 (how you will know your goal has been achieved). Once you have reviewed it, find a spot where you can be still and close your eyes for a few minutes. Tune into your breathing and notice what it's like today. Feel what's underneath you as you breathe and your body melts into its physical position with each breath. If there are any thoughts in your mind, thank them for stopping by and allow them to move on.

Shift your focus into your imagination where you can see the goal as if it's already been accomplished. Allow your imagination to paint the picture of this outcome and let it come to you unedited. Be as vivid as possible. Imagine the colors in the visual getting brighter and the feelings more intense. See if you can imagine your goal's fulfillment being as good as it can possibly get.

Notice whether there's anyone near you—any animals or plants. Is there a taste to this outcome? A texture? Anything you're touching? What about the feeling of your clothing? What colors stand out?

Listen to what you can hear around you, as well as in the distance. See this imagery and turn up the volume so it becomes the most vibrant experience you've ever had. When it feels as good as it could possibly get (or even better), take a mental snapshot and imagine turning it into a photo you can hold in your hand. As you inhale, imagine that you float above yourself, holding onto your photo and passing into the future as far as you want. Allow the timeline to come to you. Your subconscious mind can take you on a journey, and when you know you're at the perfect time for this photo, drop it and watch it land at the exact time this outcome will happen.

Imagine turning back and looking at the timeline. Notice any events between then and now that are realigning themselves so the path leads straight to this photo. Take a moment to feel grateful and comforted that you have aligned your life to lead straight to your goal. Now the only possibility is for this to become a reality for you; maybe even sooner than you think.

Take one more deep breath and scan the horizon of the timeline up to your photo, and in your next breath, allow yourself to return to the present. Start to feel your body again, and when you're ready, open your eyes.

Now you have dropped the goal into your future path, and you'll soon find yourself in that photo —but it will be your real life! You have created the perfect environment for your brain, your body, and your behavior to align with what you want. Congratulations on reclaiming your power!

The Point

Though you cannot necessarily change your memories, you can use your imagination to change the emotional attachment to them. Instead of triggering panic, anxiety, depression, fear, or other stressful feelings from our pasts, we can choose to feel strength, curiosity, neutrality, or any emotion we like. Besides, it's fun to create your own reality and know you will receive real-life health benefits! Goodbye, haunting past; hello, desired future!

The Invitation: hiStories

The Info

Humans have been telling stories for all of history. It seems as though we don't know how to exist without them. They are the roads we travel to reach each other. Every thought and opinion we form exists within the context of a story. We don't just experience stories in our brains, but through our bodies as well! It's exciting. Here's how it works:

Beginning: We meet characters and identify with their similarities to us. As we watch or hear their interactions with other characters, our brains release oxytocin. This is the same chemical released when we bond together through long hugs, giving birth, orgasms, and even imagining being close to someone (see The Invitation: Use Your Imagination).

Brain cells called mirror neurons cause us to connect to stories. These cells fire when we take action and when we watch someone else performing an action. If I watch someone score a touchdown or ride a horse across a battlefield, my brain fires as if I am the one performing these actions. When you watch a car race, you may notice yourself starting to lean the direction you want the car to go; when you see someone else laughing or crying, you may have strong urges to laugh and cry along with them; your mouth may water at an Instagram food post. The storyteller and the story listener are both activating the same parts of their brains, connecting to one another through oxytocin.

Middle: In the middle of any good story, there is a conflict or problem for the characters you identify with and are invested in. There is some form of villain or situation that threatens your new friends, which causes cortisol to release into your body. You begin to agonize over what will happen to the characters. Your shoulders may tense, your palms start to sweat, your heart races, and/or your breathing becomes shallow as you watch in anticipation. Your body is bracing for a threat that is coming from the story, not from your life.

Cortisol heightens our attention to permit quick responses to stimuli. You now have a focused anxiety mixed with the care chemical, oxytocin. You are biologically hooked into the story. You can't stop watching or reading, so you cringe while you peer at the screen through your fingers, or you stay up all night to finish the book despite knowing your alarm will sound in four hours. We've all been there.

End: A story's ending produces another chemical response. If the ending is happy, we release dopamine. Humans love a happy ending for this reason. You've likely also experienced the disappointment of a cliffhanger or a story that ends unhappily. We are left unsatisfied, negotiating for a sequel or new development, because there is discomfort within us and dopamine that we are craving.

When we experience this cocktail of cortisol and oxytocin, research shows we are much more likely to change our behavior.[12] We use stories to get people to buy things, to advocate for healthcare services, to donate money to charity, to vote, and more. Our brains and bodies will fill in the backstory of someone we are talking to in order to develop empathy because we are using it to make a decision; do we want to buy

---

[12] Jeremy A. Smith, *The Science of the Story,* (California, Berkeley, 2016).

from them, vote for them, spend time with them, listen to their advice, allow them to care for our children, and more?

Throughout our lives—whether we know it or not—we are listening to stories and using them to make decisions on our own behavior, as well as telling stories so others behave in a way we desire.

The Experience

Choose a family member you want to know more about. If you don't have a family member, choose someone you consider a mentor or close friend. Consider some important aspects of your life and what questions you would ask to learn those things about someone else's story. Contact them and ask if they would be willing to sit down with you to answer some questions about their life, because you want to get to know them better. Then follow through!

Here are some example questions:

When did the internet come into your life, and how did it change it?

Who was a mentor of yours when you were a child or young adult?

What was the most impactful gift you ever received?

What was the most important lesson you have learned so far?

If you could tell your (insert your age)-year-old self something, what would it be?

As a kid, what did you want to be or do when you grew up? What is similar to that about you now? What is different?

Tell me a story that captures the essence of you.

Alternative Experience:

Choose a younger family member (or someone you consider family) and ask to share a story about your life with them.

The Point

Stories shape our decisions and affect how we interact with each other. How we listen to and share stories impacts our entire lives in an evolutionary way.*

*For the dark potential of stories, see The Invitation: Re-Humanize

The Invitation: Love as a Verb

The Info

Humans are biologically wired to connect and interact with each other. Even you, introverts. If you don't believe me, go back and read The Invitation: hiStories again. Historically, humans have always lived in tribes and groups. A simple concept of evolution is that our bodies experience pain as a message not to do something again, because it threatens our survival. If we consider this concept in connection with others, we can understand that, for our species, relationships are critical despite being difficult and often threatening. Long ago, when we hunted and gathered together, if we were ostracized from our group, we would almost certainly die.

We still ask ourselves today, is connecting with others worth the risk of rejection? Rejection could mean the end of a relationship, but it shows itself in many forms: avoidance of certain topics of conversation, absence from important events, ignored calls or texts, or, these days, even declining a friend request online. We ask the same question about romantic partners, parents, our in-laws, our own children, our friends, coworkers, and practically any human with which we spend more than a few minutes. Some people feel a sense of safety with strangers because the chances of seeing them again are slim. If you've ever lived in a small town, you intimately understand the risk of rejection for the opposite reason—you will most likely see everyone in that town again, and if you are rejected once, you are likely to experience the same feelings of rejection again.

We don't often recognize social pain aside from physical

harm. One indicator of this is that our justice system consistently punishes acts of physical violence but is inconsistent—at best—at giving the same consequences for social and emotional harm. However, social pain can impact us in very similar ways. Rejection activates the same areas of our brain that physical pain does.[13] Even pain relievers like Tylenol can ease social pain just as they do a headache, for example. Our physical and social pain tolerances relate to each other and increase each other when used together. Though people who have lost a loved one are twice as likely to experience depression as those who have not, a person who has experienced social rejection is 22 times more likely to develop depression, and the onset is faster.[14] It is hypothesized by some professionals that bodily-based chronic pain with no defined cause (such as fibromyalgia) is linked to social pain early in life.

We know relationships can hurt us, yet we often believe we can shrug off emotional pain more easily than physical pain. We use trite phrases like, "time heals all wounds," "what doesn't kill us makes us stronger," or "this too shall pass," to name a few. These phrases are created to make us feel more hopeful about our future, but they aren't exactly accurate. Social pain comes with emotional effects which are processed through our bodies. Time and stoicism do not process emotions and can lead to further damage if we adapt to them by developing anti-social behaviors or avoid engaging relationships to protect ourselves.

---

[13] Matthew Dahlitz, *The Psychotherapist's Essential Guide to the Brain,* (Queensland, Australia, Dahlitz Media, 2017).
[14] Matthew Dahlitz, *The Psychotherapist's Essential Guide*.

We often pretend we do not need anyone in order to protect ourselves from being hurt and rejected. Instead, we can use tools to prioritize and strengthen relationships so we can increase our ability to give and receive love in ways we—and our loved ones—will recognize.

The Experience

This is a very simple practice that will change your relationships immensely. Whenever you can, start each conversation with a reminder that you care about the relationship you have with the person. If it is a difficult conversation to have, begin with a question to encourage mutual sharing.

1. Every time you greet a person you care about or want to have a healthy relationship with, begin by expressing your appreciation for them and highlighting your connection.

Example: *When you walk into your home at the end of the day, before you ask how your roommate is doing, say, "It's great to see you."*
Example: *Let your friend know your relationship matters to you before you share about your kids. "I feel so lucky to get to see you (or talk over the phone) and spend time together."*

2. Before you have a difficult conversation, establish the foundation that your relationship is of primary importance. Follow with a question so the other person knows you want to have a conversation together rather than "talking at" them.

Example: *If your child is late for curfew, begin the conversation with, "I'm glad you're home. Your safety matters to me. What happened, and what does safety mean to you?"*
Example: *Before approaching a difficult conversation about finances, remind your spouse of something about them that you are thankful for: "I feel so grateful to have a partner who wants to communicate in healthy ways with me. What is your first financial priority for us?"*

3. Difficult conversations in your professional life can be approached the same way.

Example: *Though you may be tired, enter your job and greet your coworker with gratitude: "It's rough coming in on Monday morning! It really helps me to show up knowing you are going to be here with me."*
Example: *Tell your client or patient, "I know showing up to these sessions isn't always easy, and I admire your dedication. It's one of the things I enjoy about working with you."*

4. Do this even if you don't feel motivated! If the relationship is not your favorite, this will help improve it.

Example: *If you don't like visiting your in-laws, let them know your dog is excited to see them. "When Sparky was in the car and saw your street coming up, he started wagging his tail and jumping all over! I think he is excited to see you."*

The Point

Everybody experiences social pain, and acting stoic or apathetic in relationships is a defense mechanism to avoid being hurt. The only healthy way to get through this is to look honestly at the pain and do the (sometimes uncomfortable) work of building and prioritizing relationships in our life. As our social skills increase, it will become easier to let go of the barriers we put up between us and our loved ones.

The Invitation: Stop Fire + Rewire

The Info

Trauma not only wires your brain to work differently, but it also changes the size and shape of it. A few weeks into pregnancy, a fetus begins developing the brain; the majority of development occurs in the womb. During the first five years of life, our brains develop rapidly in size and matter. Throughout early adolescence through age 25 (at least), we develop primarily in our prefrontal and parietal lobes, which are the middle-to-front sections of our brain. While development happens primarily in the early stages of our lives, we know that plasticity—the ability to change how our brain works and even the size and shape of it—continues throughout our lives. This means that stress, especially from early life, impacts how we think, feel, and behave for the rest of our lives; however, we have the capability to unwire, rewire, and change our brain function at any time.

Our brains are changed by trauma in three main ways: we have a harder time thinking logically and compassionately, we have a harder time regulating emotions and focusing, and we have an easier time feeling fear and entering survival mode.[15] Our bodies help us detect danger and manage emotions through the limbic system. Two parts of this system in our brains are the amygdala and the hippocampus. Our amygdala is the "fight or flight," responder. It is located near the brain stem and its job is to detect danger and keep us alive. When we experience trauma, the amygdala efficiently takes energy from

[15] Bessel, *The Body Keeps the Score.*

the rest of our brains and uses it to fight or escape a threat. When we experience chronic stress, the amygdala becomes more active over time. The more stress we feel, the more we practice living in survival mode. Like anything we practice, we become experts at it, and we begin to live in a state of constant panic and danger—whether it is real or perceived—in a pattern created by trauma.[16]

The hippocampus and the prefrontal cortex are less active when we are in survival mode. The hippocampus manages emotions and memory. The prefrontal cortex is responsible for logic, problem-solving, creativity, and empathy. We need these areas of the brain to focus, respond healthily to emotions, and connect socially in a positive way. When we aren't using these areas due to chronic stress, they weaken and physically shrink over time.[17]

As we live with chronic stress or trauma, we become overactive in fear and under-active in emotional control, problem-solving, and connection with others. When the stress comes from a relationship—as it does with abuse, neglect, grief, and other interpersonal trauma—we can be triggered by or avoidant of others. This is especially difficult for those of us who experienced trauma during times of rapid development, either in utero or during childhood.[18] However, healthy interpersonal connection is the medicine we need to recover.

Trauma often teaches us to escape from our bodies

---

[16] J. Douglas Bremner, MD, *Traumatic Stress: Effects on the Brain,* (Maryland, U.S. National Library of Medicine, 2006).
[17] Rajendra A. Morey, MD, MS et al., *Amygdala Volume Changes With Posttraumatic Stress Disorder in a Large Case-Controlled Veteran Group,* (Maryland, U.S. National Library of Medicine, 2012).
[18] Bessel, *The Body Keeps the Score.*

because we feel unsafe in them (see The Invitation: Move to Release). We learn not to trust or even feel our intuition, sensations, and emotions. This becomes an obstacle to connection with others. The best place to start for those of us with traumatic histories is to connect with our own bodies and rebuild safety without overwhelming ourselves so our brains can rewire outside of fear. Over time, we can feel safe in our bodies, then safe with other people. In short, trauma impacts our ability to function, but we have the power to rectify it.

Mindfulness is a great way to practice these feelings of safety within our bodies and simultaneously change the function and structure of our brains.[19]

The Experience

Disclaimer: It is common to feel uncomfortable during mindfulness practice, but if you go beyond uncomfortable into feeling overwhelmed at any time, stop the exercise and take a break to do something soothing. You can come back and try again later or reach out to a professional for support in growing your mindfulness practice.

There are many types of mindfulness. This is just one experience you can do for only 5 minutes a day to get you started or keep you practicing and seeing results. Don't have five minutes? Do it for just one!

The 5x5 in 5 (minutes)

Wherever you are, pause for a moment and become

---

[19] Jenna E. Boyd, MSc et al., *Mindfulness-based Treatments for Posttraumatic Stress Disorder: A Review of the Treatment Literature and Neurobiological Evidence,* (Maryland, U.S. National Library of Medicine, 2018).

aware of your body. Notice any places of tension and breathe into them. Observe 5 things from each sense: what you can see, hear, smell, taste, and feel—this could be something you are touching or something touching you, like the breeze.

Any time you are distracted by a thought, simply return to the practice where you left off or start again. Everyone gets distracted sometimes; the more you notice it is happening, the more mindful you become. Sometimes we think we can't practice mindfulness because we can't make our thoughts stop, but this is not true. Disruptive thoughts will occur, but as you practice refocusing your attention and reconnecting with yourself, you take control of your thoughts. The more you fail, the more you practice; the more you practice, the more you succeed. The only way to truly fail at mindfulness is not to practice it at all.

The Point

Just like broken bones, your brain can heal differently in structure, shape, or positioning depending on treatment. After significant stress or trauma, your brain can be repaired and rewired. Connecting and feeling safe with ourselves will help manage our unrest and ease us into healthy relationships with others. Trauma deeply impacts the way we think and behave, but it does not have to stay that way forever. Recovery is possible.

The Invitation: Re-Humanize

The Info

Systems are how we make sense of the world: categories, patterns, and society. We form legal, political, educational, economic, social, and healthcare systems in developed (and even underdeveloped) cultures. Theoretically, if we run them well, these systems provide structure that serve us and meet our needs.

We use statistics first to measure and predict trends and determine how to distribute resources, then to analyze the results. We create labels to clarify who the system works for, discuss our target demographics, and make sense of complex concepts. Labels save time, create common language, and can even provide a sense of belonging.

This is a soothing and lovely experience when we choose a label together, but when we don't, it can work against us to create competition, isolation, and hatred. There is a process we implement to separate ourselves and withhold compassion from others. You may be thinking, "If I don't care for someone, there is probably a good reason for it!" To this I say: Absolutely. This rationalization is the process we go through, and it starts with our language.[20] We use labels to separate ourselves from a person or group; for example, the term "redskin" was used in the 1720s to describe Indigenous North Americans. Regardless of how this term was intended, the label "redskin" separated groups of people and later gave permission to call Indigenous women "squaw." Similarly, the term "negro" permitted later use

---

[20] Brené Brown, *Braving the Wilderness,* (New York, Random House, 2017).

of the derogatory term "nigger." These words divided us into groups of people, and that is the first step towards dehumanizing each other.

Communion is our natural state. Humans are social animals, community creators, and we have evolved to interact intimately with each other. To isolate ourselves or ostracize others, we must create the illusion that we are somehow separate from them. Language is the doorway to the myth that we are different. When we read stories, we develop associations for the villains so we can see them as different from us. In the example above, we used skin color to divide groups of people. Simple labels override our instinct for connection and grant us permission to embrace the illusion of a villain that we want to (at best) control or (at worst) destroy. The stories we tell ourselves are powerful.

We dehumanize people when we categorize and label them. Historically, we have grouped people by factors such as their skin color, their gender, their beliefs, their sexual orientation, their abilities, or mistakes they have made. We believed these factors denoted subpar people. We told ourselves this story: *If "they" are free to interact with "us," our group will be tarnished. For "our" protection, we must control our social environment. To that end, we have the right to enslave people, segregate, keep internment camps, put children in boarding schools, ban cultural spirituality, and force religion.* We created emotionally and physically unsafe environments for certain groups of people, and it all started with language.

We experience this on social media and in conversation around your meal tables. As soon as someone labels themselves as a certain political party, we have the entire script of character development already in our minds of their values, morals, and perhaps even what kind of distasteful coffee they order in the local cafe each morning.

We experience this in simple ways as well, such as in professional sports. As soon as someone labels themselves as a fan of the opposing team, we have permission to call them a loser or state that now it's a war, which implies they are our enemy.

This is dehumanization. It begins with a label and ends with violence, whether physical, verbal, emotional, digital, domestic, and more. It can be subtle and difficult to identify or catch before damage has been dealt. The power of a label that dehumanizes exists in context. We must be careful of any story we tell ourselves behind a label that separates us from other humans.

Our culture often paints perpetrators as repulsive, inhuman monsters. "I could never do that" is a comforting lie we tell ourselves. The truth is, we all have parts of us that—in the wrong circumstances—can become violent, fearful, desperate, and manipulative. If you see yourself as incapable of making huge mistakes, are you really being honest? The survivor and the perpetrator come from the same paradigm. We survive by learning the same manipulation, the same pain, and the same fear our perpetrators are acting from; in that way, we can see ourselves in them. This is not to say we all end up choosing the same behaviors, but if we want to truly end abuse and the pain we cause each other, we have to re-humanize perpetrators and see them beyond their behaviors—as people. This is a big task and the reward is just as extraordinary: fewer people experiencing abuse.

Re-humanization does not have to happen face-to-face. Sometimes the healthiest thing we can do (for us and the perpetrator) is stay out of each other's lives. We can choose to re-humanize from afar or we can work on re-humanizing those with whom we don't have a history of pain. In this way, we can work together to reach each other and unlearn our toxic patterns. The following exercises will help us begin.

The Experience

Re-Humanize in 3 Steps:

1. Choose a person you dislike or someone who has harmed you.
2. Ask yourself what you have in common with them. The answer could be as simple as having the same color eyes or enjoying chocolate cake. If nothing else, a powerful observation is that each one of us suffer. If you cannot think of anything else you have in common, know that you have both felt pain before.
3. Explore how it feels to belong to the same group as this person. How does it change your perspective? What does this mean for your relationship moving forward?

As you wrestle with this, consider this: is it fair to ask someone to humanize us if we will not humanize them?

The Point

When we give ourselves permission to separate from others through the language of labels, we also give ourselves permission to be cruel. If we truly want to live in a world where our systems serve us rather than separate us, and if we want to stop cycles of war, abuse, suicide, and other epidemics, we have to take responsibility for changing the way we dehumanize people in our own experiences. Ending the cycle of dysfunction on a grand scale requires us to first end this cycle within ourselves through deep humanity, humility, and empathy.

The Invitation: Boundaries

The Info

Establishing boundaries is a common topic in the field of personal development. Though we routinely discuss how to create them, stopping there causes us to miss the part that actually protects us—keeping the boundaries in place when they are tested.

Boundaries prioritize the longevity and health of the relationship over the ease of the moment. It can feel uncomfortable to ask someone to treat you a certain way, but without boundaries, relationships are doomed to corruption by pain, mistrust, and resentment. Before we decide what our boundaries are, we need to be clear on what we want. Do we want to build or end the relationship? If we are setting a boundary after we have been hurt by someone, it's important to decide whether we are seeking validation for our pain before we end the relationship or to continue the relationship with new understanding. Sometimes we fall into the trap of believing we need to set a boundary when, truthfully, we don't want to continue the relationship. When this is the case, it doesn't matter what boundaries are set; they won't feel good because we still want to be away from the person. It's okay not to want to be around a person and to choose that when possible.

Some people remain in our lives because of circumstances outside our control, such as working with them or having had children with them. In these cases, we can establish strong boundaries to create a healthy experience for everyone involved. Please note: family members do not automatically get to stay in your life. The fact that someone is your family member does give them a free pass to hurt you without consequence. If they don't respect your boundaries and you have an unhealthy relationship with them, you are allowed to end it if that is what you want.

Contrary to popular belief, boundaries help us love unconditionally. Conditions are about the other person, but boundaries are about us. It is a subtle but essential difference, because it avoids sending the message that the person is not worthy of our love unless they behave a certain way. We don't unconditionally love behaviors; we love people, and people are not their behaviors. If we love a behavior, it is because we crave an outcome—that is a business arrangement, not a relationship.

For example, telling someone we will only spend time with them if they stop drinking places a condition of sobriety on our relationship with them. Telling them we will not be around them while they are drinking sets a boundary that protects us and preserves the health of the relationship.

The following experience will help you clarify your desired outcome and break the cycle of backtracking on boundaries and experiencing the same hurt and frustration.

The Experience

Create a boundary. You can use this template if you want:

When ______________ (previous or possible future situation) happens(ed), I (may) feel _____________. From now on, please ______________________ (state what you want instead).

1. Journal and consider what will happen if you follow through on this boundary.

2. Use your answer from #2 and ask, "Am I doing this to myself?"
Example: *If I set this boundary, the person might not want to be my friend and may abandon me. Have I been abandoning myself in any way?*
3. Ask, "If I were loving myself, what would my boundary be?"
4. When we fear an outcome, we sometimes avoid looking at it. Follow your fear and consider the possible consequences by asking, "If I set this boundary, what is the worst-case scenario?" Then, "If that happens, what will I do?"
5. Double-check your boundary by asking, "Does this facilitate connection?" Your boundaries are always about protecting you and building connection.
6. Adjust your boundary as necessary.
7. Practice saying your boundary out loud. Role-play what it will be like to talk about it in real life. Notice your tone of voice, body posture, and language; these can be whatever is most genuine for you.

The Point

Boundaries grow in direct correlation to the amount of love you have in your relationships. In other words, the more love you practice, the stronger and clearer your boundaries will be. Though boundaries allow you to love others better, they are established and upheld as a means of self-care, not for the sake of anyone else (although everyone is cared for when you care for yourself).

The Invitation: Compassionate Community

The Info

There is a silent, lethal epidemic in the United States. If you've read this far, you know human beings are wired for connection. Research shows we can maintain between 100 and 200 total relationships, and experts recommend maintaining a minimum of three-to-five close relationships to promote our optimal wellbeing. Our health is greatly impacted by our 15 closest friends and family members.[21] Collected data shows that the number of people who claim they have no close friends is rising, and zero is the most common answer when we are asked how many confidants we have.[22]

If you are feeling lonely, you are not alone. At least 40% of Americans report feeling lonely as of 2010.[23] This is not only a painful experience, but also a threat to our health. As we explored in The Invitation: hiStories, part of our survival depends on our communion with others. Loneliness signals to our bodies that we are in danger. Research shows that living with loneliness increases our chance of an early death by 45%.[24] We hide our emotions in isolation instead of connecting with community, and it is killing us.

---

[21] R.I.M. Dunbar and Susanne Shultz, *Evolution in the Social Brain,* (Liverpool, UK, University of Liverpool School of Biological Sciences, 2007).

[22] Miller McPherson, Lynn Smith-Lovin, and Matthew E. Brashears, *Social Isolation in America: Changes in Core Discussion Networks Over Two Decades,* (California, American Sociological Review, 2006).

[23] Brené Brown, *Braving the Wilderness.*

[24] Julianne Holt-Lunstad et al., *Loneliness and Social Isolation as Risk Factors for Mortality: A Meta-Analytic Review,* (California, Association for Psychological Science, 2015).

The other day, a friend said he admired that I don't settle for superficial relationships and instead consistently show up in a vulnerable way to seek out those who also want deep connection and authenticity. For me, it isn't about settling. It's bigger than that. I am fighting for human life to continue in a meaningful and fulfilling way, as our nature dictates.

The Experience

Consider the following questions to identify the types of individuals you want to find or attract to your community. Focus on meeting one person at a time.

1. What does community mean to me?
2. What does community look like?
3. What is the most important thing about community to me?
4. What am I grateful for?
5. What am I proud of?
6. What am I scared of?
7. How do I know when I am cared for?
8. How do I know when I am caring for others?
9. What activities reflect the above values?
10. Where do people who share these values spend their time?
11. Who do I already know that might have similar values (even if they have different opinions)?

Begin by reaching out to one person and invite them to spend time with you to do something meaningful. Consider telling them directly that you want to create deeper relationships and connected community to see if it's something they are interested in exploring with you. To begin the conversation, you can ask a question from the list above. If you value communication, this is a great place to start.

The Point

Whether you believe loneliness will kill off the human race or not, it's biologically proven that we are healthier and more fulfilled when we maintain meaningful relationships. Filling our lives with physical, emotional, and spiritual connection is worth the risk that vulnerability requires. Without community, our human experience is incomplete.

Acknowledgements

This book is first and foremost a love letter to my younger self. Several years ago she told me she wanted her story to be told because she couldn't do it at the time. The small child version wanted to understand what healthy love and family looked like. The teenage version wanted the opportunity to be angry in the context of her story and feel like those emotions of rage were valid and they mattered. She wanted to forgive herself for not speaking out. For much of my life I felt too scared to tell the truth and this book is for every previous version of me who was silenced by shame. Without the many versions of me over time, there is no story. I love you all and we share the truth together now.

This book is also a gift to my grandfather, Ralph Smith, who did not always teach me lessons from love, but taught me a lifetime's worth about love nonetheless. Like the last words I said to him, my intention was to honor his story in this book, as it is a part of my story as well. I never believed we would arrive in a space of love, yet by some miracle and a lot of hard work we got there. I learned to believe in the most unbelievable, to have precise and indestructible boundaries when necessary, and to feel safe without hiding from him. Because of you, Grandpa, I know what it truly means to love unconditionally.

To my parents, Clayton and Michelle Smith, who have always loved me the best they could with everything they've had. Our experiences have been complex over the years, just like any parent-child relationship is. I deeply admire the way you both have shown up when it feels uncomfortable, shameful, or just sucks. I am proud of the way we have learned to work together and to remember our relationship comes first. I have learned compassion, creativity, and loyalty from you. More than learning from you, however, I have enjoyed learning with you and hope we continue to be the best of friends for a long time to come.

To my non-biological sister, Lyssa McCall, who has listened and shown up for me since the day I met her. You have literally driven miles to rescue me when I was stranded, taken me into your family, into your home, and walked with me through the entire process of this book. From when I considered if writing a book was a possibility and not a distant dream, to the dull tasks of creating timelines and outlines, to celebrating every paragraph written until what felt sudden, a book was written. You witnessed my story before any of it was written in these pages and before the end had revealed itself. I am grateful for your sisterhood, for the reminders that people needed this message, and for borrowing your strength when I didn't have my own.

A special thanks to my cosmic companion, Nicholas Krause, who the universe gifted me at the exact moment this book rapidly took form. You showed up without reserve, dove deep and suddenly into the philosophy of what this story meant to me, and most importantly boldly loved me through every step. Your belief in me and your confidence in the significance of my work turned lonely days of writing into tender human connection. Thank you for challenging me in a way that created more freedom and love than I could have imagined.

To my brilliant editor, Hannah Luera: I knew that day we drove to church together that you would be the only person who could edit my story. The depth of forgiveness you have mastered and your faith in Spirit, as well as humanity, inspires me everyday. Not only have you made my words understandable and my grammar prettier, you committed to upholding the moral of my story in ways many editors may not have understood. We created more than a book, more than a piece of art, but a message of hope and humanity that can live on long after us. Thank you for your purposeful encouragement, for matching my fast pace, and for being truly human in our work together.

To Patricia Kane, who loved me in all the ways I couldn't ask for through the hardest parts of my childhood, you taught me I was worthy of love. Without knowing, you kept me safe and changed what would become the path of my adulthood. You have impacted what I see as important, how I love, and how I have recovered by coming to work in the classroom everyday and seeing me. I think of you everyday, I love you, and I will never forget you.

Thank you to my family Kay Smith, Corinne Smith, David Biggs, Clinton Smith, Cody Smith, Danielle Ishmael-Smith, Fallon Smith, Everly Smith, and David Biggs for being irreplaceable in my life and story.

Thank you to my Brazilian family Luciane Mariano Zenevich, Ronni Zenevich, Gabriela Zenevich, Leticia Mariano, and Elaine Mariano, for taking me in, loving me, and teaching me humanity across cultures.

Thank you to all of the teachers who came before me. They include (and are not limited to): Brother Asaiah, Nancy Vait, Rita Pfenninger, Duncan Wanamaker, Atz Kilcher, Saundra Hudson, Eva Saulitis, Tim Daugherty, Deb Lowney,

Mark Robinson, Nancy Lander, Paula Koch, Rosanne Pagano, Jon Kulhanek, Amanda Miller, Luke Gamble, Caitlin Gamble, Arthur Clauss, Kent Friesen, David Hayes, Adi Shakti, Staraya McKinstry-Robinson, Robin McAllistar, Willy Dunne, Rob Wiard, Annie Wiard, Josh Reyling, Cherokee Hope, Danny Hope, Kathryn Hunt, my friend from the driveway Virginia, and all my former students, clients, and patients, young and eldered. You are my educators, my coaches, my neighbors, my lovers, my friends, my children, and sometimes you are strangers I meet only once. Whether I liked you or not, embraced or resisted the lesson, or recognized the delivery, I have gratitude for the learning. I would not be here without you. May we collect wisdom and dust, together.

CPSIA information can be obtained
at www.ICGtesting.com
Printed in the USA
BVHW082357030120
568574BV00003B/16/P